A BRIGHTLY

GUIDED LIFE

A Brightly
Guided Life

HOW A
SCIENTIST
LEARNED
TO HEAR
HER INNER
WISDOM

Ingrid Honkala Ph.D.

TABLE OF CONTENTS

*I dedicate this book to each and
every one who helped me rediscover
the true essence of who I am.*

Foreword

TO WHOEVER is holding this book, "Hi!" I am Mike, Ingrid's husband, and yes, I am depicted in the later chapters of this book. Although most forewords are written by famous authors who will wax philosophical about the depth and insight of their protégée writer, I am not one of those. I am not a famous master who would guide you to surrender your skepticism and justify everything in this book so you would believe it. My intention in writing this foreword is only to give you a glimpse of the Ingrid I know through my experience, and who modestly skims through her life in the pages of this book.

I met Ingrid in Tumaco, Colombia when I was in the US Navy. Before we were sent there, we were briefed about the situation in Tumaco and in the country in general. According to the intelligence brief the area of Tumaco was just barely one step above Mogadishu, Somalia. At the time of our first date, Ingrid had seen and experienced about as much combat time as most special operators in the US military, yet she was very humble about her time living there. My admiration and respect towards her kept increasing as I realized that she had risen to the top of her field as a marine scientist despite living in a war-torn, male-dominated, class-separated society.

Ingrid's amazing resilience is a testament to her strength, courage and profound beliefs, and has carried her to some amazing places all over the world. To me her resume reads like an Einstein protégée, working with private and government organizations like NASA and the Navy, writing more scientific articles and books than most of her peers, presenting her research work on mangrove ecosystems and the effects of climate variability in the ocean to well-known organizations, and receiving many awards and recognitions for the high quality of her work and dedication.

Ingrid also shares my habit of wanderlust. Every year when she goes abroad to work on oceanographic surveys, I check where my little *wifita*, as I call her, has gone off to. I'm soon greeted with photos of her in all kinds of temples across the world. Most folks would probably freak out about it, but with her ability to connect with people and to pick up languages like most of us change clothes, I don't worry too much.

After reading this book and knowing Ingrid for more than fifteen years I can say that this book is a modest account of her life and experiences. In my thirty years as a special warfare combat crewman and years working overseas, I have never met someone so full of love and compassion, yet still so grounded in the world.

When I met her, my personality was very dark — I was on my way to writing my own demonic resumé. But Ingrid burned that out of me, just by being the loving, kind and joyful person that she is. Today I am trying to follow her example. Little by little, I am learning to shine from within and bring a spark of light not just to those around me, but into some of the darkest areas of this earth.

So go ahead and read this book now. It will help you open your mind to different possibilities, and to shine your light as you reconnect with your inner wisdom. — *Michael M. Honkala*

CHAPTER 1

Falling Into Darkness

IN SEPTEMBER 1973, when I was nearly three, I fell into a reservoir of water located on the patio of the house where I grew up in Bogota, Colombia. This cement tank, about five feet deep, was above ground and held 900 gallons of frigid water. Bogota is a high-altitude city that can be quite chilly in the morning, and the water in the reservoir might have been below forty degrees Fahrenheit. The purpose of this deep tank was to collect water for hand-washing clothes, so next to the tank there was a small flat surface for scrubbing.

Early one morning after my parents had left for work, I and my two sisters Lis and Lili, none of us over three, were left at the house in the hands of the maid. She was a young lady who didn't pay much attention to us when my parents were not around. That morning my oldest sister and I decided to play catch across the tank. The walls of the tank were high for us, so we grabbed some stools and managed to pull ourselves up. My sister sat comfortably on the flat surface next to the tank, and I kneeled precariously on the thin edge at the other side, so I had to make an extra effort to keep my balance.

What happened next still is so vivid in my mind that I can remember every detail, like it happened yesterday. My sister and I were playing with two medium sized balls, one dark yellow and the other green. The balls had the letters of the alphabet engraved on them, next to pictures of an animal or an object. We were throwing the balls to each other when the yellow ball slipped from my hands. I tried to grab it but it rolled on the surface of the water. Then I lost my balance and fell into this dark and seemingly bottomless hole. My eyes locked onto the picture of a smiling white bunny painted on the ball as I was falling, and I can still feel the texture of the letters slipping through my fingers.

The first feeling of the plunge was a shocking coldness. My body convulsed violently, and it felt like my chest was imploding. My desperation was intense, as I couldn't breathe. When I touched bottom I instinctively thrust upward with my feet, but I rapidly sank again and then my body became unresponsive. I could hear my sister screaming distantly from the surface, trying to reach me, but there wasn't anything she could do; she was too little to reach me. I could feel my heart pounding in my head like a base drum; with eyes open, I stared hopelessly into the darkness.

Then suddenly came a feeling of total relief. I didn't know why then, but I was at peace and there was no anguish. My heart stopped pounding; everything turned absolutely still; I was no longer cold and didn't feel like fighting anymore. My body simply became insubstantial. Then I noticed that a dim light, like a candle, had somehow begun glowing, just enough to illuminate my watery surrounding. I could see little bubbles, and then behind them I noticed a body suspended in the water. I remember looking curiously at its expressionless face and seeing the eyes staring, wide open.

This was my own lifeless body, but I was neither surprised nor frightened to recognize it. Instead I felt an immense joy and freedom, and soon the image of my body was replaced by the most beautiful flowers blooming from nowhere. And before I knew it, I was somehow being lifted and carried away by the flowers.

In hindsight, it's no wonder that I was relieved to be freed from the burden of my body, as I was a very fragile and sick baby and always felt unwell. As the mysterious flowers lifted me away, every-thing felt peaceful and bright; at last I was free from the aches and pain I had carried since birth. So I simply kept going away without ever looking back at that body.

I then abruptly found myself in the maid's bedroom, looking down on her lounging on the bed. She was listening to the radio, unaware of what happened to me. Next, I was looking at my mom walking down the street several blocks away from the house, coming up on her bus stop. Time and distance had vanished for me; I could be anywhere at any time. It wasn't until that moment that I realized that I didn't possess a defined form. I could communicate with everything and I was part of everything. It was like the Wholeness and I were one. As I sank into an atmosphere of pure bright light I had the clear awareness that before I became human, I was a being made of pure light, just as I was now.

While I was experiencing this blissful state of being, my mom suddenly sensed an intense feeling of dread. She turned around and ran back home, as fast as she could; when she came into the house she knew exactly where to go. On the patio she found my oldest sister leaning into the tank, helplessly wailing to her, "Ingrid is in there and I can't reach her!"

When my mom pulled my lifeless body out of the water, several minutes had passed. My lips were blue, my body cold, my skin pale and I had no pulse. She was trained in CPR so she pushed her fingers into my little chest and blew air into my lungs until I began choking and gurgling. I don't remember feeling anything when she was trying to revive me; by that time I was far away. Suddenly I was falling, as if I had jumped from the top of the tallest high-rise in the world, feeling as if I was being sucked back into my body like it was a vacuum. Then came the return of the intense, agonizing cold, I knew that I was back.

When all of this happened to me I was just a baby. I didn't have any preconceived notions about a near-death experience (NDE). At the time I was too little even to understand that I had essentially died. All I knew was that I'd left my body and went to a place of indescribable well-being. However, this experience didn't feel unfamiliar to me; somehow I comprehended that the current life that I was living was just a continuation of a very long existence.

As I grew up and remembered my drowning, I could never get away from the question, "How could I have seen my body lifeless if I was still alive?" This experience made it clear to me that there was an existence beyond the body. Like the shell of a crab is an extension of the crab itself, our body is also but a shell, and when it is not needed it will fall away. Before I was three, I was gifted with knowing that I had existed for a very long time. In fact, I have come and gone in different realms many more times, wearing many different shells.

CHAPTER 2

The Beings of Light

FOR ABOUT A year after my young near-death experience, often while falling asleep, I started seeing colors, hearing sounds, and feeling motions like the ones I experienced during my drowning. Time would start to slow down, then abruptly speed up. It also felt as if for an instant I was being taken somewhere else, then I'd experience a vacuum inside my belly and chest while being pulled back in. This feeling was disturbing indeed, but it came with a glimpse of a dimension I had been part of, and wanted to go back to. I was completely unaware at the time that I was having out-of-body experiences.

Over time the length of these journeys increased, and the uncomfortable feeling of falling back into my body simply vanished. The dramatic changes in colors, sounds and movements persisted but they stopped bothering me. In fact I looked forward to them, because they opened the door into a very serene place where I felt completely calm, free and safe.

Since my NDE my health had deteriorated; I refused to eat and often felt upset. I would look at myself in the mirror, scratch my face, and pull my hair out while hysterically crying. Then I would run to my mom and scream out loud, "You don't understand! I am not this person, this is not me, this is not my name. I should not be here!" Patiently she would hug me, wipe away my tears and murmur, "Don't say things like that, you are a smart and pretty girl. God has given you this life and you should be thankful." Since I wasn't able to communicate my feelings in a way that people could understand, I became frustrated and increasingly isolated myself from the world. Most of the time I just wanted to be left alone. My sisters were too young to understand what was happening, and my parents were too busy working and trying to survive day to day, so they did what they could to deal with a very challenging situation.

Thankfully, the help that I needed arrived in a most unexpected way. Right after my fourth birthday, during one of my vivid journeys, I was surrounded by star like figures of pure light shining everywhere. They were of different sizes and the colors were mostly white, silver and gold. Suddenly, one of them, shining in pure gold, shaped itself into a human form and moved toward me until I sensed its touch. Feeling absolutely astonished I said, "Wow! You are a Being of Light," and then I snapped awake.

Afterwards I kept seeing the lights frequently while sleeping, so I became eager to go to bed. During some of the visits, many of them would be shaped as humans; others remained shapeless bright light. It was chiefly the golden ones which adopted human form; on very rare occasions blue and silver transformed. Regardless, I knew that each of them was a Being. Each time that we were together I sensed the deep feeling of joy that one can experience upon returning home after being homesick for a long time. I always felt more peaceful and healthier, and began interacting more with my family. I told them that I felt good because I was meeting Beings of Light while I slept. My parents felt relieved because I was sleeping well, feeling better and having good dreams.

For a while I could only see these beings when I went to bed, but before long they started to appear anytime, anywhere. The first time I saw one with my eyes open, I stood in the shower, relaxing as the water washed over me. Suddenly, an intense and astonishing blue light flashed on before me, staying for a few seconds before it vanished. Even at four years old, I knew it was a Being of Light.

I felt both thrilled and peaceful at the same time. They kept reappearing often, sometimes bringing with them the delightful fragrance of flowers. They didn't say or do anything in particular, but they were so stunning — and I felt so loved in their presence — that nothing more than their presence was needed.

I first heard them talk after I threw a big temper tantrum. Since my NDE I didn't identify with my name, and sometimes I felt bothered about people calling me Ingrid. That particular day I got very angry at the maid for calling my name repeatedly. I turned to her and said, "Don't you understand, that is not my name!"

"Okay, so what is your name?" she replied exasperated.

"I don't need one," I answered, then got very mad and walked away crying. That night as I fell asleep the bright golden Being of Light embraced me and I heard a voice talking in a very loving and clear manner. "It is going to take a while for anyone around you to understand."

"Understand what?" I asked, feeling confused and astounded.

"Understand that your True Self does not need a name. As you are discovering, names are not needed in the realm of the Light."

"You're right!" I affirmed.

"All things that you are experiencing," the Being continued, "and the ones that you will experience, are all gifts given to you to help yourself and others."

"I don't understand; how am I helping anyone?" I asked. All I'd been hearing from people was that my behavior was not helping.

"More than you imagine," it answered. "But don't worry because eventually everything will be clear to you, and you will be able to communicate with everyone in a way that they will understand. For now, just stay calm and don't mention this conversation to anyone because they are not ready to understand. Remember we are here and you can talk to us; we are always listening."

Still, it was hard for me to understand why nobody could understand me. Why did I feel so peaceful with the Beings of Light, but so uneasy when surrounded by humans? I couldn't understand why this was happening to me, to which the Voice simply replied, "Because you are special and you are beginning to know it."

Then I said, "What do you mean that I am special?"

"Everyone is special, but they don't all know it yet. Just remember you are not alone and you will meet people to help you walk your path, so you do not need to worry."

Then all was quiet. After receiving this message I felt a lot calmer, and even though things were not still clear in my mind, I didn't need to ask any more questions. My tantrums stopped and for a while I felt at peace. But the question of "Why me?" continued to resurface throughout the course of my life. Only when I was a little older could I understand that the Beings of Light had started to teach me faith and trust. All problems could be resolved if I'd just allow myself to rest calmly in the caring hands of Divine Guidance; but I was very resistant, and that resistance would bring a great deal of pain in my life.

CHAPTER 3

I Was Not the Only One Feeling Different

EVEN BEFORE my near-death experience I was never an ordinary child. Due to the peculiarity of my behavior and fragile health, an atmosphere of family troubles always revolved around me. During the first two years of my life I was constantly ill, never spoke a word, and seemed absorbed in my own world. I could drift off for countless hours contemplating a piece of lint, an insect, or a spot on the floor, and often I would simply stare into the air, lost in my own mind.

Then one day, when I was nearly two, words started to stream out of my mouth clearly and fluently, I knew so many words and could speak in sentences so well that my parents and relatives reacted in stunned disbelief. Suddenly I wanted to know everything, explore everything, and ask every question I could imagine. I could do things that were well beyond my age: drawing and painting pictures, building things, and putting together complex puzzles.

I also wanted to know how everything worked, so I attempted to dismantle a few electronics around the house including the family television when I was four. I was very intrigued to understand how this device could hold people inside. Thankfully my mom discovered me when I was opening the back with a screwdriver, and warned me against breaking anything in the house. Still, when I received the first Christmas gift I ever really wanted — a radio — my first question was, "Can I get a tool to open it?"

I wasn't interested in playing with dolls, fascinated instead with Legos, blocks, train sets, and a microscope, among other things. I also had a photographic memory, making it very easy for me to retain information. Learning to read, write, do math and engage in problem solving was not a challenge for me while growing up. Although my learning abilities were astonishing, my social interactions were far from the normal, and suffered even more after my NDE. I just didn't feel attracted to interact with most people, especially kids my age, whom I didn't want to connect with. During break time at school I used to sit by myself and build something, draw, contemplate nature or communicate with the Beings of Light, whom by now were part of my daily life. Every once in a while I would play with my sisters at home or school.

At the age of five, when I was in kindergarten, a teacher noticed that every one of my paintings featured auras painted around objects, animals and people. I was not coloring outside the lines, since the colors around the figures were clearly different. There were also multiple renderings of sun like symbols, usually yellow, but sometimes blue or silver. The teacher asked, "Are those things the sun and the stars?"

Without thinking I answered excitedly, "No, they are all of my friends."

Looking confused, she inquired, "What do you mean?"

"They are not things," I explained, "They are the Beings of Light who are my friends." The teacher looked shocked, so I sensed that talking about this was perhaps not safe. I went quiet. She wanted to know more, but I crossed my arms and refused to talk, especially after she threatened to call my parents. Feeling upset and perplexed, I began to wonder if there was something wrong with me. I always seemed to be the cause of adults worrying.

After this incident the teacher decided to arrange a meeting with my parents as soon as possible, but due to the short notice only my mom was able to come. The teacher announced that she was worried about me, and that it was important that they work with me to improve my social skills. She thought that I was talking to imaginary friends. When she showed the aura paintings to my mom they stared at them for a while in silence.

I tried to explain: "You know, Mom, these are the colors that we wear around our bodies, and those are my friends." My mother looked directly at me with big – stop talking mom eyes; her expression was so intensive that I immediately stopped talking. Then she addressed the teacher and said, "Don't worry, we will work on it, everything will be alright. This must be just a phase." My mom didn't show much concern in front of the teacher, and after a few more minutes we left.

On our way home while sitting on the bus, as I was feeling low and staying quiet. My mom held my hand and suddenly broke the silence by saying, "I do believe you." I almost jumped out of my seat with excitement because I had my mom's approval, and I didn't want to be in trouble. Then she continued: "I too, have the ability to see things that others cannot."

Feeling excited and confused I asked her, "What is it that you see?"

"I see what people call spirits."

"What are spirits?"

"They are the souls of the people who have left this world," she answered.

She then told me that seeing spirits had frightened her very much when she was little, but she learned to manage and live with it.

"But Mom, I am not afraid," I said, thinking that the spirits and the Beings of Light were the same.

"That's a good thing," she said. "There's no reason to be afraid, but everyone reacts differently."

"Why can we see things that others can't?" I wondered aloud, still confused.

"Because we are special," she replied. "These are some of the gifts that God has given to us, that make people like you and I different and unique. However, I learned from a very young age that my family and teachers couldn't understand what I was talking about. They seemed frightened and called me a liar, so I learned to keep quiet to avoid getting into trouble."

At that very moment I felt as if the Beings of Light were talking through my mom, reminding me how special we were and that it was best for now to remain silent. I also remembered that the Beings of Light had said that some people would be put on my path to help me. So that day, despite feeling sad because I saw myself as even more different from others, at the same time I also felt relieved. It was calming to make a deeper connection with my mom, and she relaxed because she recognized my unique nature.

Later that night in bed, feeling restless, I asked the Beings of Light a question I had put to my mom earlier: "Why do we have to be aware of being special, if that makes other people feel frightened?"

By now I had learned that the Beings of Light had different ways to answer my questions. It could be through sound, images, or sensations. This time the soothing voice of a Being of Light answered, "It's natural for most human beings to be frightened of anything they cannot explain, especially the adults because their minds have become mired in what they consider to be normal.

Anything out of the ordinary feels threatening and scary to them…"

"You are not really different from anyone, you are just aware of what other people have forgotten. Remember, everybody is special but not everybody knows it yet. The time to remember will come for everyone. Don't worry, for you are not alone, and that's all you need to know now."

Feeling better, I finally fell asleep. However, the unforgiving environment of school would keep reminding me over and over again how different I was. No matter what my mom or the Beings of Light said to make me feel at ease, I'd never entirely escape the burden of feeling different.

CHAPTER 4

When I Doubted That My Mom Loved Me

THE HOUSE I grew up in was divided into two parts that were given to my dad and uncle by my grandfather. The first floor was given to us and the second floor was given to my father's older brother Danilo, who was married to my mom's sister Teresa. Since we were all so closely related the two families decided to leave a little passage in a wall connecting the two floors. The passage was so small that we called it "the hole." Aunt Teresa was a stay-at-home mother, who was a very bitter and vindictive person. She was especially focus on trying to sabotage my mother's life at every turn. Both my parents worked so we were left in the care of the maid, or as a last resort my aunt.

One day I was sitting at her kitchen table watching as she decorated a cake when she looked at me, shook her head and said, "Ingrid, I feel so bad for you that I have to tell you the truth."

"What is it, Aunt?"

"Forgive me for what I am going to tell you," she smirked, "but you need to know that your mom doesn't really love you," she blurted. "That's because you are not your dad's daughter," she sighed.

This comment was followed by a detailed comparison of my physical appearance to my dad and my sisters, telling me how much I didn't look like them. My dad was a very handsome, blonde, blue-eyed guy, and my two sisters were such beauties with big, green eyes and light colored hair. In Colombia it wasn't common to see blondes, so it already was evident to me how their beauty captivated everybody. I was the only one with dark curly hair and dark brown eyes. According to my aunt, that meant I wasn't pretty like my sisters. My mom also kept my hair short, so after touching my head my aunt continued: "How could she possibly love you? Look at how she keeps your hair! She only sees you as someone so simple and unattractive. Poor little Ingrid," she sighed again.

Speechless, with tears in my eyes, I touched my hair and looked down as she added, "Don't waste time asking this to your parents because they will deny it. I am telling you the truth because I care about you. If your mom truly cared about you she would never leave you at the care of maids, especially the one that almost let you die when you were younger."

Then she hugged me and said, "Come on, stop crying and help me finish this cake. I am here for you, unlike your mother." After weeping for a while longer while helping my aunt finish the cake, I went home and cried alone for hours without telling anyone why. Since I already felt different from almost everyone, my aunt's comments were very convincing to a five year old.

Feeling dejected, I asked the Beings of Light, "Why do I have to be so different that nobody loves me?" That night while falling asleep the only thing the Beings of Light whispered was: "Everything is going to be alright."

"How?" I cried. "I hate my life, I don't want to be here."

My sisters heard me crying and asked, "Are you okay?"

"I am fine, just leave me alone!" I shouted. I couldn't understand how everything could be alright, since I had just learned that I wasn't my father's daughter and my mom didn't love me. Nothing made sense, especially because I had felt close to my mom. But my aunt had managed to poison my mind and now I was filled with resentment and doubt.

From that day forward I wanted to leave the house. Every time my mom would get mad at me for any reason I would go to my bedroom, pack a little bag and threaten to run away. She'd get very angry and I would end up going to my bed crying.

A couple of weeks later after my aunt's revelations, an unexpected visitor arrived — one of my father's half-sisters named Irmis, whom he hadn't seen for years. She lived in Venezuela and didn't like to travel much, but after many years of being away from Colombia she wanted to see her family. This was the only time she would ever visit our house, where she stayed for only four days. On the second day, I threw one of my tantrums about running away after arguing with my mom. My parents didn't have an idea of what was really happening, so they decided they would send me away for a little while with my Aunt Irmis with the intent that I would stop misbehaving and learn to appreciate our home.

After my parents gave me the news, I went straight to Aunt Teresa. "See, I told you!" she exclaimed. "This proves that she doesn't love you and now she's going to get rid of you."

After my early near-death experience, I became very aware of not feeling strongly attached to anything or anybody. Thinking that my mom didn't love me made the decision to leave with my aunt Irmis very easy. I also liked her right away, so two days later I was gone.

I really liked my Aunt Irmis' big, airy two-story house with so many rooms to explore. In a first-floor shop she sold all kinds of office supplies, and since I loved art this was like heaven to me. My Aunt Irmis was always very busy, so I spent long periods of time alone painting and wandering around the house.

After a few days, I had explored every single space in the house, finding a secret sanctuary. It was a very small patio at the end of the house, hidden behind a little wooden door that looked like a secret passage. This small and dirty patio, entirely made of cement, was the home of two big, old and mean German Shepherds. The dogs were allowed in the house at night to serve as guards.

At the beginning my Aunt Irmis didn't have any idea that I was visiting her ferocious dogs and freaked out when she found me one night petting them. After I proved to her that they liked me, she agreed that I could be with them under supervision, which I promptly ignored. Two more people lived in the house with my aunt, but since everybody was busy I could sneak my art supplies onto the patio.

There I felt secure with the dogs and strongly connected with the Beings of Light; I could clearly sense, hear and see them shining all around the patio. I wondered how could anybody be afraid of the Beings of Light and these "pretty puppies." I'd always felt comfortable connecting with animals, including the so-called "scary" ones, such as rats, moths, and frogs. It always amazed me how people could despise these animals, because where others saw ugliness or felt fear, I saw beauty and felt love.

At the time I felt surrounded by so much human anger, hatred, distrust, and sadness that I preferred to be peacefully surrounded by animals. After all I was born in a very violent country (Colombia was declared one of the top ten most dangerous places in the world at the time) and belonged to a middle-class family struggling to survive the horrific effects of a country at war plus the intense drama of the day-to-day life. Once on the patio, while feeling so close to the dogs, the Beings of Light told me:

"There is so much good in the world of humans. Being human is a great path of learning; every single experience brings about growth and evolution. And you have the power to bring the good out of people."

"How come?" I asked, feeling shocked.

"Someday you will discover this power within you."

"Will you show it to me?" I questioned.

"You already have it. You'll see it for yourself."

However, being only five I couldn't understand what they were talking about. I didn't feel comfortable around people.

At the beginning I enjoyed being in my aunt's house and rarely asked for my family, but as time passed I started to feel very melancholic about not being with my family. For the first time I wished I could be with my sisters playing together. Only about a month had passed, but it started to feel like if it was an eternity. I wondered if I would ever return home.

As two more months passed my sixth birthday was approaching in November, I became really anxious. My parents always held the family birthday party because my two sisters and I were all born in November. I wanted to be with them to celebrate together. Every time I talked to my mom on the phone I would tell her how ready I was to return. She would try to comfort me with sweet, loving words and then make excuses about my father being close to finishing law school and getting a new job requiring a lot of travel, while she was very busy working and taking care of my sisters.

I got very depressed and my aunt started to worry. Now more than ever I didn't want my Aunt Teresa to be right. I decided to write my mom a letter. I grabbed a sheet of paper from my aunt's shop that happened to have an angel painted at the bottom and wrote:

"Please Mom, I beg you to come and get me. It hurts badly to be away from home. I promise to be good. I will be like an angel. I truly miss all of you, Ingrid."

When my mom got the letter she couldn't stop crying, and declared to my dad that it was time to bring me home.

The day before my sixth birthday, my dad flew to Venezuela to pick me up. My heart was bursting when I saw him entering my aunt's shop, and I ran to him and hugged him. When I arrived home I was very excited to see my mom and my sisters, and I could feel their happiness about having me back home. This was the first time I felt such joy with my family.

I was also astonished to discover that my mom was seven months pregnant. When I left she was skinny, and now she was enormous. Feeling quite shocked I asked, "How did this happen?"

My parents laughed so hard it made us all explode in laughter. Seeing my family so joyous was something new to me. It was one of my best birthdays.

Not long after returning home I told my mom how hard it was for me to be gone. She explained to me that big suffering could bring big rewards. "Look how happy everybody is, including you, since you returned."

Christmas was approaching and I could see clearly how my family, especially my dad, looked happier than ever before. The best gift I could have that Christmas was to be altogether. The New Year brought great changes into our home, including a newborn baby. When my mom called from the hospital I didn't care to know about the sex or health of the baby; all I asked was, "What is the color of the eyes?"

"They are brown, just like yours," she answered.

After a deep sigh of relief, I asked, "Is it a boy or a girl?" The most important thing for me was to know that my new baby sister, named Fabiola, looked like me.

The next amazing change happened not long after the baby was born at the end of January. My mom hired a new housekeeper, Leonor, who came to live with us and became our loving protector. She established a close friendship with my Aunt Teresa's maid, learning about all the abuse that my aunt and the previous maids had done to us. We never told anything to my parents because we feared the maid's and my aunt's reprisal, thanks to Leonor all the hidden truths were revealed to them.

My dad had to travel a lot, so we didn't see him very often. It was during a weekend visit that he learned the truth about my aunt's abusive nature. He was furious and went upstairs to my aunt's house, where they had a huge argument. After coming downstairs he sealed the hole that connected the two houses, and Aunt Teresa never hurt us anymore.

It is amazing to think that my aunt's malicious plan to turn me against my mother turned into a very significant event in my life, since being away from my family gave me the deepest sense of connection and love for them I'd ever felt. For the first time since the near-death experience, I felt that I belonged somewhere in the world of humans. My attitude became more open and loving. After all the Beings of Light were right when they said to me, "Everything will make sense, everything will be alright."

However, I couldn't understand how my Aunt Teresa could hurt me. "Wasn't my aunt supposed to love me?" I asked, feeling resentful.

At the time I couldn't disagree more with the Beings of Light when they answered, "She does love you, but she doesn't know what she is doing. She is here to teach you."

"What can she teach me by being mean?"

"That is not what matters; just look how joyful you are with your family."

At only six, I couldn't see that the Beings of Light were trying to show me that in the end, all the challenges in life bring us closer to our heart.

CHAPTER 5

Living with Spirits
and Talking to Slugs

AFTER WE had been living in our house for about five years my mom decided to paint it, with the help of her younger brother since my dad was working out of town. One night after painting for hours, my mom and uncle decided to quit for the day. Since it was late my uncle stayed overnight. My mom, my sisters and I had been sleeping in the only bedroom that had not been painted yet because the smell of the paint was very strong. So, that night, my uncle joined us in the same bedroom and quickly fell asleep. My mom closed the door of our bedroom and left the doors of the rest of the house open so the rooms would get good ventilation while the walls were drying.

Late that night when everybody was sleeping, I awoke, startled by a presence violently entering the room. I didn't recognize this presence as anything that I had witness before, but as soon as it entered, the whole room turned into shadows as the auric light around my family and all objects dimmed. The presence was a deep black silhouette, and even though I couldn't see any facial features, I knew it was a man. I felt petrified, and terror engulfed my entire body — I was literally paralyzed.

The man was wearing a large coat, big heavy boots, and a

sombrero. He was tall and appeared strong. His movements were not gentle and I could sense that he was in a bad mood. I wanted to call my mom and uncle for help but I couldn't talk or move. In silence I pleaded to God and the Beings of Light, "Please protect me; don't let him know that I am seeing him." He left the door wide open and crossed the bedroom heading to the walk-in closet. Once he reached the closet he opened the door wide and disappeared into the closet after turning off its light, which my mom always left on.

When the presence disappeared into the closet, all the auras brightened. After seeing a blue Being of Light shining next to me I was able to move again. The room was very quiet and everything was very still until I heard my mom breathing deeply and shifting in her bed. I knew she was awake, but I felt so scared that if I moved the presence would come back out from the closet, so I stayed awake in my bed, very still, staring at the Being of Light. The company of this blue Being made me feel a lot calmer.

Suddenly my mom jumped out of bed, I did likewise and followed her. We discovered that while the bedroom door had been left wide open, the rest of the doors in the house had been closed. The smell of paint was strong; I followed my mom around the house while she opened the doors to allow some ventilation. It was very early in the morning and everybody else was asleep. She whispered to me to go back to bed, but I refused and told her how scared I was after seeing a shadow entering the bedroom and disappearing in the closet. She sat on the dining room and held my face while saying, "I saw him too. Don't be afraid, he is one of the spirits that lives in this house." Then she told me that she had been seeing and sensing a few spirits since we had moved into the house.

"Mom what I see are beings that are always shining," I

revealed, "and when I am with them I feel peaceful and happy. What I saw tonight was different; it looked dark and frightened me."

"All this time I thought that you also could see spirits like I do," my mom responded excitedly, "but now I think that you are seeing angels."

"They don't have wings like in the pictures," I said.

"Perhaps you cannot see the wings, but for the way you described them they must be some kind of angels. Perhaps your guardian angels..." With tears in her eyes she added, "You are so lucky for being able to acknowledge their presence. God must have something special reserved for you." Going from feeling scared to overjoyed, I answered, "I call them Beings of Light but I don't mind calling them angels."

My mom then told me that the dark spirits were not bad and would someday find their way to heaven. She told me not to tell anything about this to anyone, especially my sisters. "Remember when I told you that not everybody understands, and besides I don't want you to be in trouble at school," she reminded me. My mom had grown up with two demanding and very religious aunts who used to punish her harshly for doing anything sinful. Talking about spirits was forbidden.

"Mom, what can I do not to be scared of the spirits?" I asked.

"Pray to your guardian angels every day. They'll protect you and take your fears away," she replied. Then she taught me a short and beautiful prayer to the guardian angels. My sisters learned it too, and we repeated it every night before going to bed.

Although I started to feel better, the peace didn't last for long.

One week later, on a very cold night, my mom put us in bed with some extra blankets and we said our prayers. In the middle of the night I was awakened by the feeling of something very cold that grabbed my right ankle and stanched me out of the bed. Petrified, I laid on the floor while the force kept holding my ankle. It all happened instantly. I couldn't see the entity but I sensed that it was the same one that I had seen before. Although I was horrified, this time I was able to yell, "Beings of Light, Angels, please help me!" My ankle was released and I screamed for my mom's help as well. She ran into the room and found me lying on the floor, unable to move. She picked me up and put me back on the bed.

By then my sisters were awake and wanted to know what was happening. My mom said that everything was okay, that I had just fallen out of the bed.

"I didn't fall, Mom, somebody pulled me out," I sobbed.

Taking me out of the bedroom, my mom told my sisters, "She just had a nightmare, go back to sleep."

Once in the kitchen I told her all that had happened and asked her, "Mom, why is this happening?"

"I have realized that every time we make changes or a visitor stays in the house, the spirits get disturbed," my mom explained. "But I was the only one seeing and sensing them until now," she admitted.

"Why me, Mom?" I wondered.

"I don't know. But one thing I know for sure is that we should pray; God will protect you as he always has protected me."

Not being able to avoid feeling upset, I kept crying as we prayed together. "Mom, I don't know if praying helps," I interrupted in a whisper, "because we did it before going to bed and look what happened." Then I remembered: "But calling the angels was different. It definitely helped, because right when I called them the dark spirit went away," I added.

"Praying and calling with faith is the same thing," my mom

answered. "You just have to really mean your words when you are praying to God and the angels. When you have faith you are truly trusting God."

That night I went back to sleep with my oldest sister Lis, still feeling distraught. I asked the Beings of Light, "What is wrong with these spirits?"

After their soothing light brought me to peace they answered: "Nothing is wrong; they are just like us. Although they left their human bodies, some of them still have a keen interest about the matters of this world. They have forgotten who they truly are and feel lost, but sooner or later they will find their way home."

"Why do we have to live in this house with them? What do they want from us?" I asked.

"You can help them," the Beings said.

"How?"

"Just pray for them."

"The way my mom taught me?"

"That's right," the Beings agreed, then explained further, "The light of your presence is all they need, trust us as your mom said. Don't be afraid, we are always with you."

"I know," I said, feeling relieved. "My mom calls you angels. Is that what you are?

"People call us different things, you can call us whatever you want," they whispered softly then slowly disappeared.

From that day, I started to pray with deep meaning, feeling that God and the Beings of Light were protecting me and helping the dark spirits find peace. However, the experience of being snatched out of the bed had been so intense and terrifying that I found myself sleeping in a tight fetal position for a long time. Eventually my faith grew stronger and the fear went away, because after that night the spirits never touched me again.

My mom and I couldn't keep the secret about the spirits from my sisters for long. During the fifteen years we lived in that house all of us, including the maids and some relatives and friends, experienced many more encounters with them. Still, no one ever mentioned seeing or sensing the presence of the Beings of Light. I always wondered, *Why only me?*

The Beings of Light would say only that eventually everyone would be able to see them. To avoid getting in trouble or being ostracized at school, I decided to follow the advice of my mom and the Beings of Light, never talking to anyone outside our family about them or the spirits.

* * *

Our house had a large patio, next to the bedroom I shared with my sisters, where I could often see spiders, slugs and other little creatures moving around. Since the birth of my third sister, my parents thought that the living space in our house was too small and we needed to build one extra bedroom to accommodate everybody. The baby slept with my parents until she was about seven months old, when they decided to use part of the patio for a new bedroom.

As a disturbing side effect of the remodeling process slugs started coming into our bedroom, and they crawled into my bed because it was the closest to the door. Almost every night when I went to bed I would find slugs meshed within my sheets. So at night my mom and I would check the bed, making sure that nothing was there. Still, sometimes in the middle of the night I'd be awakened by slimy slugs crawling on my body. Distressed, I would call my mom for help. I always had an enormous love and respect for nature, so I would ask my mom to help me to take the slugs away without killing them.

One night at bedtime, after following the routine of checking the bed, I asked my mom, "Why is this happening only to me?"

Sensing my pain she looked me in the eyes with compassion and said, "Remember when I told you that praying and asking with faith is the same thing!"

"Yes Mom, I do," I replied.

"Okay, so talk to the slugs; ask them to leave. Tell them that you love them but you would prefer that they don't come to your bed anymore. Tell them that they do not belong there."

After a brief silence, she added, "Have faith and be patient because it might take some time to persuade slugs."

Convinced of the truth in her words, I talked to the slugs with the absolute assurance that they could hear me. Kneeling next to my bed after doing my nightly prayers I said:

"Little slugs, I truly love you but you should be on the patio where you belong. With all my heart I ask you to please not come back to my bed. I promise that I will continue protecting you and visiting you on the patio."

I repeated these words for several days without fail and one day, like a miracle, they were gone. After finding the bed free from slugs for a couple of days, overjoyed with emotion my mom said, "See! I told you to have faith."

Filled with joy, we celebrated with my sisters by hugging each other and praying together thanking God. As my mom was leaving the bedroom I saw the very bright light of a silver Being of Light shining next to my mom's shoulder. Then the memory of a sentence the Beings of Light repeated often to me came to my mind, "Everything is alright."

I giggled and shouted to my mom, "Having faith is when you

know that everything will be alright, isn't it?"

"It is kind of like that; you put things in God's hands and they get resolved. You just have to trust."

Once my mom left the bedroom, excitedly I said to the Being of Light, "The slugs listened!"

In a blink of an eye it moved next to me and said, "Of course they did. When you are one with the Whole there is only one language... Love." Then it disappeared in a flash.

My sisters, thinking that I was talking to them cheered from their beds, and then we all went to sleep.

That's how, at the age of six, I started to realize that there was a real power in praying and in this mysterious thing that everybody called faith. So I began to develop a devoted practice of praying. Since I was raised as a Catholic I repeated all the Catholic prayers I learned from my parents and at school. I prayed for the wellbeing of my family and the people, spirits and animals in need.

CHAPTER 6

Brownies and Chicken Soup

MY PARENTS never had a lot of extra money to spend on our education but because of our family connections we were allowed to attend a very prestigious Catholic School in Bogota. During first grade, after lunch most kids would line up to buy treats at the school's convenience store. I never cared about food until the day I saw a group of girls buying and enjoying a batch of fresh-baked brownies. The look of ecstasy on their faces after every bite brought me to have cravings for the very first time. Penniless, I waited in the cafeteria until it was almost empty and timidly I approached the lady at the cash register and asked her, "Could I get one of those brownies, please?"

"It is three pesos," she grumbled.

"But I don't have any money Miss," I said.

"No money, no brownie," she boomed then stomped away.

Once at home I asked my parents if they could give me money to buy a snack at the school's convenience store, to which they replied that they didn't have any extra money and had already paid for my monthly school lunch program. I wouldn't accept *"No"* for an answer, so I needed to formulate a plan to get that brownie. I couldn't understand why it required money. *There has to be another way*, I kept thinking. That night while I was taking a shower, a blue glowing Being of Light appeared in the bathroom. As a plan started forming in my mind, I whispered to it, "I am going to get that brownie, but don't worry I know what I am doing." Without responding, it simply disappeared.

The next day I woke up ready to execute my plan. I spent the lunch break in the cafeteria where I waited until the school bell rang, announcing that the break was over. After seeing that there were some leftover brownies, I discreetly unlocked one of the windows in the cafeteria and went back to class feeling excited. I waited patiently for the long school day to end. As the bell rang for the last time, I joined the crowd of people leaving the classrooms. Once in the corridor, with my heart pounding in my chest I hesitated for a second, but then I sneaked into the bathroom and remained hidden in one of the stalls until everything was in complete silence.

Nervously and cautiously, I left the bathroom and went to the cafeteria where I pushed the window open. I quickly entered the room and went behind the store's glass shelf to find the brownies. I felt relieved, and forgot about the world when I saw and finally held in my hand one of those brownies. I dropped myself on the floor and ate it with complete delight. One brownie was all I needed. For the first time ever, I felt good eating something.

Once I finished eating and I was out of the cafeteria, I executed the rest of my plan: going to the nun's housing and asking for help. I knocked on the door and one of the lesser Sisters who I recognized as Sister Patricia opened it. "What are you doing here?" she asked in surprise. I explained to her that the bus had left me when I was in the bathroom and that I was going to need a ride home. She called Sister Julia, another lesser Sister and together they decided not to bother the Mother Superior and started to search for my parents' information. They called their office numbers with no luck, so they suggested waiting for them to call and asked me if I'd like to build some puzzles.

The Sisters treated me with such kindness that I couldn't contain my guilt and after a short time being with them I confessed everything about the brownie, despite being very afraid of getting punished. They didn't approve of my plan, but since they came from impoverished families they could sympathize with my situation and were so moved by me telling the truth that they were almost in tears, as I was in tears too.

"You just needed to ask for what you wanted," they suggested.

"I did but nobody listened," I sobbed.

"Here is the deal," one of them said. "If you promise to never do it again we will keep this secret." After I gave them my promise we all prayed together. Then they even asked me if I wanted another brownie!

Not long after my father called and was on his way to the school to pick me up. On our way home while sitting in the back seat of the car and listening to music, a golden Being of Light appeared next to me. "Telling the truth requires a great deal of courage. Good for you," it said in a very soft and loving manner.

"Thank you… I just felt so guilty about lying when the Sisters were treating me so nicely," I whispered.

"You should value your determination, but you do not need to take anything by force. Life is always giving, and what is meant for you will come to you. Look, they even offered you more brownies."

"For free!" I added in amazement. "I knew that money was not the only way. However, what I did to get the brownie felt pretty scary."

"Always say and do what feels right. Trust your heart instincts and if anything feels frightening or uncomfortable then that is not the way."

That day I began to recognize that being honest was actually powerful, but I also decided that I was never going to give up what I wanted, no matter what. Nevertheless, as the Beings of Light said, I had to learn to get what I wanted by following only what felt good within my heart. That way I would not have to suffer bad feelings of guilt and remorse. Overall, that day I was glad not to be in trouble, and grateful because I was able to enjoy the best brownie of my life. I never stole anything at school again, and the sisters never reported me to anyone.

* * *

About a year later, I was sitting in the school's cafeteria, ready to eat lunch, when a plate of chicken soup was set in front of me. Since I had a very strong connection with animals, I completely freaked out when I saw the head, beak and legs of a death floating chicken in my bowl. Frantic, I shrieked: "There is a chicken in my soup!" All the kids sitting around started to laugh and make fun of me. I immediately hid under the table and only came out when forced by Mrs. Sandra, a third grade teacher. I was so devastated about the death of this chicken.

Sitting alone at the principal's office where Mrs. Sandra took me for throwing this tantrum, I quietly cried to the Beings of Light, "I don't want to eat animals." For only an instant a golden Being of Light appeared in the room and said, "You don't have to eat them." Feeling relieved I thanked it and from that day, at the age of seven, I completely stopped eating meat.

After the experience with the slugs my love for animals had grown even stronger. I would bring home any bird, frog, dog, cat, or mouse that I found in the neighborhood that I thought was in need of aid, and with the help of my mom and my sisters we would care for them and find them homes. So I couldn't conceive for any reason the idea of eating animals.

For the majority of the people the situation in Colombia was very difficult and the resources were short so we were taught to eat without complain. My mom managed my particular situation at home and didn't force me to eat meat, but at school it was different. When eating at the school's cafeteria the nuns and teachers wanted me to eat everything and kept repeating, "You are a bad girl for not eating the food God is providing to you. There are so many kids starving in the world and you are being wasteful. That is a sin!"

While lying in bed one night confused I asked the Beings of Light, "How come I am being bad for not eating animals?"

"Nobody is being bad. Everybody is doing what they think is right."

"Eating animals can't be right!" I protested, feeling disappointed with their answer. Then without arguing they left.

The situation at school grew out of hand, so to solve the problem my mom decided to send me to school with my own lunch. However, some teachers like Mrs. Sandra, the third grade teacher, didn't agree with my behavior. A few times I heard her saying to other teachers and students that lower class families were always a problem. In Colombia the economic classes were very divided and you were treated according to your class.

At the age of eight I was devastated when I got Mrs. Sandra as my third grade teacher. One day I raised my hand while Mrs. Sandra taught a lesson with her back to us as she wrote on the chalkboard. "Mrs. Sandra," I volunteered, "we already learned that lesson last year."

When she turned to me, the look on her face reminded me why

I always regretted speaking up in her class. I was the inquisitive and eager one, and often the quickest to learn a new subject. But Mrs. Sandra somehow felt threatened by it—to the point that I would have said she was bullying me.

"If you already know everything you can sit in that corner and let the rest of us be," she barked. Her face was contorted in a grimace that made her look less than human.

After that day she moved my desk from the front row, where I liked to sit, to the back corner of the room, and never assigned me any other work or acknowledged my presence when I raised my hand. Sometimes during class time she would put the other kids to work in groups, and wouldn't allow me to participate with the activities of the class. Even at lunchtime, since I brought my own lunch, she made me eat at my desk alone while the other kids would go to eat and play outside. At the beginning I didn't complain, because I thought that somehow this was all my fault, but after several days of getting ignored I started to feel troubled.

One morning after the snack break, feeling angry, I sat with my arms crossed at somebody else's desk in the front row. "Ingrid, what are you doing there? Go back to your desk," Mrs. Sandra shouted angrily. I refused, then she grabbed me by the arm and dragged me back to it. My classmates laughed making me feel even angrier. "Here we do what I say," she yelled. "Silence, everybody!"

I got so mad that I took my shoes and socks off and stood up on top of the desk as she walked away. All the kids burst out in laughter pointing at me, then the teacher turned around. "Ingrid, come down from that desk and put your shoes and socks back on right now." Still on the desk I said, "See, now you can see me!"

Looking enraged with anger, she grabbed my arm and forcefully took me to the principal's office. "You are in big trouble, young lady."

"You're the one in trouble!" I shouted back.

"You do not talk to me like that. Remember that I am the teacher. No one is going to listen to you. It is my word against yours. Keep it up and you will know trouble when we kick you out of school."

At the principal's office she didn't let me talk, and then they sat me by myself for a long timeout.

Back at my desk still upset, many angry thoughts invaded my head. Mrs. Sandra appeared strong, but to me she looked fragile. I could see her aura and it was very dim compared to other people's auras. *There must be a way I could hurt her*, I thought. Then the intense and bright blue light of a Being of Light flashed for a few seconds next to the teacher's shoulder and head. Then my anger stopped and all I could think now was about the Beings of Light.

That night while I lay on my bed, the Beings of Light told me, "There are easier ways to clear obstacles. If you caused her any harm, your energy would become like hers, therefore you would not be acting any different from her." Firmly they added, "It is not through pain that we alleviate pain."

"I am sorry. I tried to talk but no one at school listened. I don't know what to do," I said, feeling regretful and frustrated.

"You will find the way. Talk to the right people."

I wasn't sure what to do. Other than guide me in the right direction, the Beings of Light never told me how to resolve problems. They would only repeat, "Follow your heart instincts and do what feels good."

Thinking on Mrs. Sandra's statement about no one believing my words, I felt trapped and started to feel sick. For the next few days I developed a very high fever that prevented me from going to school. Every morning I would feel unwell, but as the day passed

I would get better. The fever disappeared during the weekend and when it came back on Monday morning, my mom asked, "Is there something going on at school?"

"Yes Mom, but I don't want to be in trouble," I said hesitantly.

"You are not in trouble; don't be afraid to talk to me. The last thing I want is to have you sick because you are afraid of causing trouble."

"The teacher said that nobody would believe me."

"When have I not believed you?"

After I told her what was happening at school, my mom said, "All of this will end today." As I was getting ready for school she told me, "Go to your classroom and wait for me there. I am going to talk to the principal first and then I will come and get you. Do not tell the teacher I am coming." I was still feeling sick and feverish that morning but I decided to follow my mom's plan without complaint.

My mom waited until lunchtime to come and get me, because I had told her that I would be in the classroom eating my lunch alone and this way she could prove to the principal that we were not lying. When I saw my mom entering the classroom with the principal, I became so emotional that I barely was able to tell the principal all the facts. When everyone came back into the classroom after the break we were waiting for them. Then in front of everybody my mom gave an incredible speech about fairness, ethics, love, and compassion — and how the teacher was lacking all these beautiful qualities. As everybody was absolutely quiet, probably feeling some guilt, my mom told me to stand in front of the class and say goodbye because I was not going to come back. At the very minute I said my goodbyes I felt very energetic and the fever was gone. That day I felt so in awe of my mom for her amazing speech, and for the courage it took to confront everyone and believe in me.

After my nightly prayer I said to the Beings of Light, "I know that you keep telling me that everything will be alright, but sometimes it is way too hard to see how that could be."

"Being afraid doesn't resolve anything, does it?" they softly whispered.

"I guess not!"

"Clearing yourself from fear is a good way to start."

"How can I do that?"

"You have been doing it all along. When you close your eyes and focus on the Light your mind becomes quiet, doesn't it?"

"Yes, it always does. It feels great! I'm never afraid when I'm with you."

"It is because fear cannot exist where there is Light."

"I see! That's the reason why being with you brings me peace. In your presence I feel loved and at home."

"That's right, in the absence of fear there's only love, and when there is love the way reveals itself… clear and easy."

That night I recognized that the big fear I had about being kicked out of school was gone at the very moment my mom told me that I wasn't going to go back. Just that fast and easy, my life situation had shifted. However, following my heart wasn't usually that easy. It required a lot of courage and determination to make the decision to break through fear, and remain consistent without giving up.

CHAPTER 7

Grandma's Light

MY PATERNAL grandmother, Lilia, was born in Bogota and later moved to Venezuela where she got married to her second husband. She loved Bogota very much and missed her family deeply, so after a few years of being gone she decided to rent an apartment in the city that enabled her to stay for longer periods of time. During one of her visits, my grandmother brought to our house a picture that took my breath away. She pulled it out of her purse and showed it to my parents while I was standing next to her. "Look, Fabio, this picture was brought from India by your sister Martha."

"Who is that, Mom?" my father asked.

"He is a Hindu Master. Your sister went to meet him in India, and now she wants to go back with your nephew Yuri to see if this Guru could somehow cure his autism."

"Why him?" my parents inquired,

"He is a very powerful Guru. That's why they show him on this picture meditating in a lotus position surrounded by a very big energy field, or what is called an aura. People believe that he has healing powers."

By now I knew what the word *aura* meant, but I hadn't seen any one with such a big one. Amazed, I asked, "What does it mean meditating in a lotus position, Grandma?"

"Lotus position is when you sit with your legs crossed like on the picture and meditation is when you close your eyes and clear your mind from all thinking."

"Is meditating like praying?" my mom asked.

"Kind of, but instead of a prayer you focus your mind on a sound called mantra."

"A sound… what kind of sound?" I inquired.

She told me to close my eyes and repeat the sound OM (*aum*) a few times. "Can you feel its vibration?" she asked.

"Yes, it feels good."

"Did you think about anything else when you were repeating it?"

"No, I didn't."

"Ok, then this was your first meditation."

"That was fun and easy!" I shouted with excitement.

"Gurus devote many hours to meditating, and by clearing their mind from unnecessary thinking they find the hidden answers to all questions," she stated matter-of-factly.

"What is a guru, Grandma?" I continued.

"A guru is a very wise and compassionate teacher, a true Master."

"What does he teach?"

"He teaches us to be mindful, and guides us to find within ourselves the true attributes we are made of, such as love, joy, peace and kindness."

My grandmother continued talking to us about spirituality, the power of the mind, healing through energy, and so on. While she was talking her aura was glowing brightly. My parents seemed interested and asked a few more questions; however, after a while they left Grandma and I talking together. I couldn't stop listening and asking questions. She was the first person I met who expressed herself in a similar way to the Beings of Light.

Grandma Lilia was raised as a Catholic, but she always had a very open mind and wanted to know more beyond the teachings of her religion; behavior that wasn't regarded with good eyes by a community of passionate Catholic followers. Nevertheless, despite the possibility of being criticized and ostracized, she started to seek other spiritual paths that would give her inner wisdom to know more about her True Self.

She joined an ancient mystical order called the Rosicrucian Order, which teaches profound wisdom enabling followers to reach their highest potential in all levels of being: physical, mental, emotional, psychic, and spiritual. She also studied different teachings of Buddhism such as Tibetan, Zen, and Nichiren.

That night I went to bed feeling excited and thinking that someday I wanted to be like that guru, so wise and wearing a huge aura. Sometime in the middle of the night I was awaken by the vibration of the sound my Grandma had taught me earlier. "*Aummmmmm...*" it lasted for a while before I heard the Beings of Light saying, "Dalai Lama."

"What is that?" I asked, confused.

"You can ask your Grandma."

During a later visit, I did ask my grandmother about the Dalai Lama, and from there we became gradually engaged in deep dialogues about reincarnation, karma, energy, the spirit, the mind and the body, which she referred to as a temple. Learning about the existence of other religions, philosophies and beliefs was like the most exciting gift someone could have given me at this time in my life.

CHAPTER 8

Playing with Fire

O N A quiet Sunday afternoon, two of my cousins and I decided to play camping. I was eight, my older cousin Andres was eleven and the younger, Carlos, was three. The top floor of their house had a big patio with one small bedroom that we chose for our campsite. Since we needed a tent we pulled the long curtain ends curling on the floor out from the windows and secured them to some chairs. Then we moved a small area rug inside the tent and made a bed with some pillows. It was a perfect tent!

After the tent was set my older cousin got hungry. "I am starving!" he exclaimed. "It's time to cook some food."

"What are we making?" I asked.

"We are making french fries, so we are going to need potatoes, a pan and some fuel to make a fire. Stay here with Carlos and I will go get what we need."

First, he got the potatoes and a kitchen knife, and asked me to peel them. Back at the kitchen he found a pan and a glass jar, and then went to the garage where he filled the jar all the way to the top with gasoline from a storage tank. While he was sneaking back upstairs my aunt saw him and after smelling the gas she took the jar out of his hands. "Where do you think you are going with that jar? I forbid you to play with gasoline!" she howled. "And leave that pan back in the kitchen," she continued yelling as she put the jar high up on a top shelf.

Andres arrived upstairs empty-handed, murmuring his discontent. I was too strong-willed to let this go, so I convinced him to get the jar back. Since Carlos needed to go to the bathroom, we found the perfect opportunity to distract my aunt. "Go and ask Mom to take you," Andres told Carlos, sending him downstairs. As they were going to the bathroom, we sneaked downstairs and managed to take back the pan and the jar filled with gasoline.

Back in the tent, feeling victorious, Andres chopped the potatoes, while Carlos and I ripped up some newspapers and put them inside of a big pot with some twigs. "Move back, I am going to light the paper," Andres said, holding some matches. As the paper began to burn he poured some gasoline into the pot, and instantly the opening of the jar caught fire very violently. Panicking, he dropped the jar on the floor and fire rapidly spread all over the rug. Andres pushed Carlos away from the fire, and while he was trying to move the curtains away from the flames, he yelled at me, "Go and get water from the tank!" In disbelief I looked at the fire consuming the rug and without hesitation ran to the nearby patio that had a deep-water tank, for doing laundry, sitting in a corner. Once there, I picked up a big bucket placed next to the tank and after climbing to the edge of the tank and filling it all the way with water, I ran back to the room and poured it all on top of the fire. In a matter of seconds, the fire was out.

There was smoke everywhere and as we were making our way out of the bedroom, crying and coughing, my uncle and aunt suddenly appeared. They had been sitting in the living room watching TV when water came dripping down from the chandelier, and smoke invaded the room.

"What is going on?!" they screamed hysterically.

"The room was on fire but we put it out," we said, crying. My uncle ran into the room to make sure that the fire was completely out. After seeing the rug, which had been turned into charcoal, he came back out looking pale.

"We could have lost the entire house and our lives by this," he moaned while coughing.

We were still crying and trembling so we all moved to the open patio to catch some fresh air. Once we relaxed a little, my uncle asked, "Why does it smell like gasoline?" Before we could answer my aunt looked at Andres with killing eyes.

"Sorry Mom, I will never do that again," he cried, as she slapped him on the head.

"Did you guys use water to put the fire out?" my uncle asked.

"Yes, Dad, Ingrid brought the big bucket filled with water," Andres answered.

"It is a miracle that we are still standing here, because you should never use water to put out a gasoline fire. It is the worst thing to do," my uncle said, holding his head. "By the way, how in heaven did you fill up and carry that five-gallon bucket full of water? It's at least twenty feet from the tank to the bedroom!"

"I don't know Uncle, I just did," I sobbed.

"That had to be your adrenaline, and the help of God," my uncle said.

Nobody was able to understand how a scrawny eight-year-old had managed to reach into the tall tank, fill up that bucket, and carry it all the way into the room to extinguish a big gasoline fire. I don't recall perceiving the wall of the tank being too high, or feeling that the bucket was too heavy, or thinking that the room was too far, or that the fire was too big.

When we all calmed down, my uncle asked if I could repeat what I had done. But when I tried, I couldn't re-enact what I had done with the bucket in just a few seconds during the fire.

"All this is God's doing. This is a miracle," he declared, lifting his arms up and looking at the sky.

Later at night once in bed, I asked the Beings of Light, "My uncle said that thanks to God and my adrenaline the house didn't burn. He said it was a miracle. Is that true?"

"Yes," I heard them saying. "Adrenaline is a powerful substance that helps humans respond to an extreme situation that requires absolute attention. Once the mind is completely focused, all unnecessary thinking is out of the way, and then the mind and body are free to express their power. In this state the mind is limitless, because it is able to connect with all the forces vibrating at the same frequency. In other words, an unlimited mind can manifest unlimited possibilities."

After a short pause they added, "We are part of that unlimited mind, so when you made the decision to put out that fire, we were there to guide you and help you. You didn't fill up and carry that bucket all by yourself, nor did you extinguish that fire alone. Because you allowed it, we were there with you all along."

"So, we are truly never alone!" I said, feeling excited.

"An unlimited mind can never feel alone, because it knows that loneliness doesn't exist."

"And what about the miracle?"

"The normal, limited mind is focused on what's seemingly impossible. Trapped by this limitation, people can't recognize all the forces at their disposal, so when something like this happens, they call it a miracle. If they could see clearly they would realize that there are no miracles... or that everything is a miracle."

CHAPTER 9

Visions

I WAS NINE years old when my dad took us to Cartagena for summer vacation. At the time he worked for the Security Service Agency of Colombia (now known as National Intelligence Agency). While working with this agency my dad had to travel all over the country, and due to the nature of his work he was often invited to interesting places. This time we visited a US Navy warship. We never had been on a boat this size before, so while on board we were very excited, looking around as we were learning about the ship's defensive capabilities. My dad was thrilled and kept asking questions. Everybody looked so proud while sharing the knowledge about their ship with us. More than being impressed by the ship, I was drawn by their passion and by the confident way they managed themselves.

At the end of the tour we encountered a Navy Petty Officer dressed in white standing at the gangway. He saluted my dad and shook his hand while my dad thanked him. My mom and sisters said "thank you" as well. I was the last in line and once it was my turn, I wanted to shake his hand too. As soon as I touched his hand, I was instantly taken somewhere else in my mind.

I was standing in an unknown place. It was a large room surrounded by columns and handrails. Feeling puzzled, I kept looking around until I saw a young, handsome guy staring at me with large piercing eyes, a few yards away at the end of a short corridor. He was blonde, with bright blue eyes, wearing a camouflaged jungle uniform with his face partially painted. I couldn't take my eyes off him. He smiled at me and said in English, "Hey it is me, I am glad to meet you."

I understood because I was learning English at school. Feeling utterly confused I asked, "Who are you?" He only kept looking at me and smiling, then I heard the Beings of Light say, "Some day you will meet and marry." Immediately after hearing these words I was back at the gangway. Feeling perplexed, I abruptly let go of the petty officer's hand and stepped back.

"Are you okay?" he asked.

"Yes! Okay! Thank you," I said with agitation, then ran to catch up with my family.

I had been having visions since my near-death experience. The Beings of Light had told me that everyone has access to the "unmanifested" as long as the limited mind is out of the way. However, I never felt so shocked about any other vision before. At this age I wasn't interested in boys at all, and seeing my parents struggle so much with their marriage had me thinking that I never wanted to get married. That night I asked the Beings of Light, "What do you mean about me meeting and marrying that guy? I am just a child!"

"As you already know, you just had a glimpse of what has been already created. Only when you are ready will it manifest," they answered.

"But, who created this one?" I asked.

"You."

"Me! When, how?"

"You were so thrilled about the people and the experience on the ship that you wished someday it would be your own reality. Now it is there and someday you will be a part of it. As we have told you before, no one else but you can create and shape your own reality. It is an ongoing process that started long ago, even before you assumed this human form."

"The people and the ship were very nice, so I don't mind that. But who is that guy? Why would I marry him?"

"You will not only marry him. He will take you to his country and you will greatly help each other and many other people too."

"At church they say that marriage is forever. If I don't like him, can I divorce him, like Grandma Lilia did?"

"You will do what feels right to you," they answered.

Their last comment made me feel better because it gave me a sense of freedom, since in Colombia at the time, divorce was regarded as sinful by the church and its followers. However, at this age I was already refuting the belief that people had to stay married even though they didn't love each other.

After the Beings of Light left, I was still thinking that it was not in my interest to get married so I decided that it was best to erase this vision from my mind. Still, an intense desire to learn English developed within me. Although I was learning it at school I never felt drawn to it before. I also began feeling very interested in the United States and its people. For the first time, I was fascinated by this subject. It was as if I had opened a door that wasn't going to be easily closed.

CHAPTER 10

The Temple

I FELT SO deeply devoted to God that at age ten, on the day of my First Communion, I thought about becoming a nun. All I wanted to do was to be with God. However, the God I sensed within myself was not the same God that the Catholic Church was introducing to me, which was very confusing.

At school we were told repeatedly that we should fear God. One night, I asked the Beings of Light, "If God is pure love, why is he so angry that we should fear him? Who is this angry guy?"

"There is no who," they answered, "there is only Wholeness. There is only Love — Love beyond anything the human mind can possibly conceive, because Love is not a thing of the mind. It can only be lived and experienced."

"God is what I sensed when I fell in the tank when I was little, isn't it?"

"Yes, *It* was as *It* is now. It is unchanged, an ever-present Love."

"I don't understand, because I don't always sense this Love. It only happened the day in the tank, and when I am with you. So how can it be always present?"

"If you look deep into it, the only time you are not experiencing Love is when your mind is in the state of fear, because fear obscures Love. Love is all there is. It is who you are until the fearful mind gets in the way, making you think something different."

"So why do they teach me at school and church to be fearful?"

"People fear what they don't know and cannot explain. Being fearful is a way to run and hide from the unknown."

"So, if I know that God is Love, then there is nothing to fear."

"That's right. There is nothing to fear," they affirmed.

After talking to the Beings of Light, the idea of fearing God, along with the concepts of sin and guilt, were something I couldn't try to believe anymore. Then I went to our church, only a block away from home, and I brought up the subject to the priest.

"Father, we should abandon all fear because fear is actually taking us away from God," I told him.

"What do you know, you are just a little girl! Life will teach you that if you defy God you will be sorry," he barked, looking distressed. "Young people are easily tempted by the devil," he added.

"There is no devil Father, only confused and fearful people," I replied.

"That is nonsense, you still have much to learn!" he yelled, his face turning red.

He looked so angry that I simply went silent. Before rushing out he said, "Sit here for a few minutes, then think carefully about what you are saying and pray to God for forgiveness."

That day I started to question everything about the Catholic teachings. Less than a year later, I had given up the idea of becoming a nun. However, all this left me with a deep sense of sorrow. I felt very lonely in this world of humans where my grandma, and sometimes my mom, were the only people who seemed to get me.

Thankfully during those days grandma stayed in Bogota longer than usual. During one of her visits I had the opportunity to share with her some of my most intimate feelings.

It was a cold and drizzly Sunday afternoon, so Grandma and I were all cuddled on my parents' bed trying to warm up. She was talking to me about the wonders of this life and how the body was a divine temple. Although her words sounded deep and beautiful, all I could really hear was my mind saying loudly how much I rejected my body and how ready I was to leave this world behind.

After listening quietly, I haltingly admitted, "Grandma, there has not been a single day for the past couple of years when I haven't thought about wanting to die."

She immediately sat up and held my hands tightly while looking at me with her big blue eyes. At first there was silence, then she continued talking about the greatness and marvels of being alive. However, soon she realized that none of that was resonating with me. After a short pause, the words that I really needed to hear came out of her mouth: "There is nothing wrong with dying," she said.

"I know, Grandma," I sighed. "My mom says that I essentially died when I fell into the water tank when I was little. People are afraid of dying, but if you want to know the truth, that day in the tank after I left my body behind, I experienced the most joyful and peaceful moment of my life. That is what I would call being alive, is to be in heaven."

My grandma closed her eyes and after a deep breath she said, "Death is part of life itself; we just think that they are separate. The end of one cycle is but the beginning of a new one. The important thing is to allow the entire cycle to reach its natural end."

I clearly understood everything my grandma was saying because I already knew that death was not the end. However, I didn't feel interested in being part of this long-lasting cycle. Then she said, "Time is meaningless if we learn to enjoy the ride with every breath."

"I have tried Grandma, but I feel so different from everybody else to the point that it hurts at times. Other than you, no one else seems to understand most of what I feel or say. When I wake up in the mornings I ask myself if all of this is a dream, and wonder when am I going to wake up?"

Although my grandma was trying to be calm and open about discussing this subject with me, she was also clearly concerned about my wellbeing, and then she asked, "Have you ever contemplated the idea of harming yourself?"

"No, Grandma, I don't want to harm myself; I just want to die," I answered. "If I die, like in the water tank, I can be back in heaven." I also told her there were only a few places where I could feel truly peaceful. One was my bed when I was sleeping and surrounded by angels (as I referred to the Beings of Light when talking to her). The other was the little chapel at school, where I used to sneak in, to hide in solitude. I deeply enjoyed the silence and serenity of this cozy space that smelled like wood and burning candles.

Since my twelfth birthday was approaching, my grandma decided to take me somewhere I could feel peaceful and serene without hiding. She hugged me and said, "Just hang in there, I am going to take you to a place that I discovered recently. When I go there I feel at peace. You are going to love it."

"What is this place, Grandma? I asked.

"It is a Zen Buddhist temple," she answered.

Colombia was a Catholic country, so the idea of visiting a Buddhist Temple was something unheard of. At first it appeared like any other of the townhouses located in a quiet neighborhood with very steep narrow roads. We parked at the bottom and set out on foot to climb to the temple. Once there, we rang the doorbell and an old lady let us in through a big wooden door. As soon as she opened the door, the sweet smell of incense reached deep into my nose. We followed the lady who took us upstairs into an open room covered with dark wooden panels, something very unusual in Colombia. The light in the room was dim, illuminated only by candles, and the space felt warm and cozy. It was absolutely perfect for me.

At the end of the room there was an altar with a golden Buddha statue and many other ceremonial artifacts. There were pillows on the floor where a few people were sitting in meditation. An older man wearing a robe welcomed us into the room, and my grandma asked him if he could teach me a form of meditation that was good for me. The monk told us to sit on the pillows and taught me a simple but very powerful meditation technique that focused on my breathing. He said, "No matter what comes to your mind, just keep your attention on your breathing. If you are drifting away, simply become aware and come back to your breathing. Breathing brings you to now, and now is all that matters."

Then he added, "Anything that was, is no more, and whatever is to come is born in the now. Be aware of your breathing, be aware of the now, nothing else is needed." As I centered my vision on a spot on the carpet and focused my awareness on my breathing, I was able to experience an incredible sense of well-being. Everything felt so natural, exceptionally comfortable and familiar.

At the end of a long lasting meditation, before Grandma and I left the temple, we went to say goodbye to the monk. I told him, "My grandma is a very busy person so it might take a while before I can come back to the temple."

He leaned down toward me and answered, "You can practice this breathing meditation wherever you are, because you already have a temple."

"Do I?" I asked.

"Yes, you are the temple. So all you need to do is to close your eyes and be aware of your breathing. That's all," he affirmed.

His teachings and his words felt completely familiar. The whole environment brought me to experience deep joy. For the first time in a long while, I felt completely peaceful and at home in the world of humans. From this day on I started to practice this form of meditation, which brought me to feel more serene and in connection with the Love that is God.

CHAPTER 11

The Four-Leaf Clovers

Y MOM moved my sisters and me to a smaller Catholic school. We liked it better because the environment was a lot friendlier, but this school only spanned grades from kindergarten to fifth. So after almost three years of being there, we moved back to our former school. My parents thought that because I was twelve by then, things were going to be easier for me. But the memories of feeling ostracized for being different came back when I met some of my previous classmates and teachers.

The only thing I liked about this school were the wide-open, grassy areas where people hung out during break time. Growing along with the grass were large patches of clovers, where someone would occasionally find a single four-leaf. Finding that special clover would bring joy to the lucky one, since that person was granted the possibility of making a wish. I never saw anything else so exciting for the kids at that school.

One day during lunchtime, I sat on the grass by myself feeling down and asking the Beings of Light, "Why do I have to be back at this place?" They didn't give me an answer, so after finishing my lunch I just remained seated on the ground looking for four-leaf clovers. My mood lifted when I found one right next to my foot. Excited, I wanted to share my discovery with someone but I didn't have any friends yet. After seeing the other kids running and playing around I closed my eyes and made my wish: "I want to have a friend here at school."

Then I was instantly engulfed by a very bright and astonishing mix of gold and silver light. It came from a group of Beings of Light, who shone intensely for a few seconds. Then their light started to swirl around and descend, illuminating the ground like a powerful flashlight, until it disappeared into the ground. As I looked down I saw a pinprick bright light, like a minuscule star, coming back up from the ground — and from it arose an amazing image of a four-leaf clover growing before my eyes. It was the most beautiful thing I had ever seen. This was followed by another tiny star shooting from the ground together with another four-leaf clover, then another and another until the whole space around me was adorned with dozens of four-leaf clovers.

I looked at the people around me, and as usual, no one else seemed to notice that a startling event had happened right in front of them. Then I heard the Beings of Light say, "The clovers are here to be shared." Elated, I yelled with excitement while pointing at the clovers: "Look, there are four-leaf clovers everywhere." The children playing nearby came to see and grab the clovers. As they were picking them up and making wishes they were thrilled, yelling at the others to come and get one.

"How is this possible? It is a miracle," they exclaimed.

"Yes, this is something magical," I replied, thinking about the Beings of Light.

That day I had all the kids around me smiling and thanking me for showing them the four-leaf clovers. Feeling grateful for this incredible gift before going back to class, I went into the bathroom to thank the Beings of Light. Then I heard them say, "Remember, your limitations are only in the mind."

That day I realized that it was actually possible to get closer and enjoy the company of my new schoolmates, but I just hadn't found the way to approach them openly. I felt so different from them that it was very hard for me to make friends. I also didn't like my physical appearance, which would make me feel very self-conscious. But thanks to the four-leaf clovers, things began to change. Soon a girl from my class became my first school friend.

I also found a lot of support from my oldest sister, Lis, who was very popular at school. She had a great sense of humor and was amazing at sports, so people wanted to hang out with her. Many times she stood between me and bullies to protect me.

Despite Lis and I being only one year apart, she knew more about the ups and downs of the world. She seemed to know everything about music, makeup, clothes, and of course, boys. I wasn't really interested in any of that but she kept repeating to me that I needed to learn these things in order to fit in. I listened to her and tried to follow her as best I could, but soon I discovered how hard it was to try to become someone different from who you really are. Although the Beings of Light had clearly shown me that limitations were in my mind, I didn't know how to be completely at ease around people who thought and behaved so differently from me.

Why was it still so hard to fit in this world? I wondered.

CHAPTER 12

NASA

I WAS always my mom's companion whenever she needed to visit someone, buy something, go to the doctor, or find a new job. To go anywhere we sometimes needed to take more than one bus. Since my mom often didn't have enough money we were forced to walk a lot. When walking with my mom we would sometimes spend the time chatting, but usually we would remain silent, immersed in our own worlds.

One day, on our way to the doctor, I was very quiet because I wasn't in the mood for walking; it was a cold and drizzly day. I was just listening to my mom's worry about ways to bring more money home. As I listened to her I kept thinking, *Why do things have to be so hard for my mom... why do we have to struggle so much for money?* Then I started to worry about myself and about my future. I started to put myself down: *What can a girl like me expect from the future, when we don't even have a few coins to pay for a bus?*

Suddenly my mind was overtaken by a vision; in a flash I was somewhere else. At this age, twelve years old, visions about the future were becoming more vivid and powerful. Some of them occurred as I was praying and meditating, but others arrived without warning. In this one, I was right at the entrance of a vast room that looked like a library. It seemed limitless. It was also quite dark and the little light entering into the room from windows close to the ceiling made the environment appear foggy. Although I saw people far in the distance, there was the quiet and peaceful feeling that one would find in a library. The more I walked into the room, the smaller it became until it was reduced to the size of an office. There were a few desks aligned in a row and the room was filled with middle-aged people, mostly men.

They were all paying very close attention to my presence. As I looked at each of them, the Beings of Light gave me a quick biography. Even though I learned that they were very highly educated, I didn't feel intimidated. Instead I felt welcomed, very secure and comfortable. As I stood there quietly we didn't exchange any words, but I felt as if we had instantly shared a whole world of knowledge. I could have stayed longer, but the vision didn't end there.

Next I was on a long, wide boulevard where the sky was bright and the air was warm. I was almost blinded by the brightness of the sky. The median of the boulevard was covered with green grass and tall trees adorned with white flowers. Feeling awed, I walked right on the boulevard, as there were no cars. I didn't see any people, but there were rows of buildings on each side of the boulevard. After passing a few, I suddenly stopped, astonished, because right in front of me was a building with the symbol of the National Aeronautics and Space Administration — NASA — on it. I heard the Beings of Light say, "Someday you will work there."

Then, I was back with my mom. We were still on the same block we'd been walking a few moments before, although I felt that a greater time had passed.

At the time one of my dreams was to become a marine scientist, so I couldn't see a connection between wanting to work in the ocean and visiting the stars. Still, the vision was amazing. As I kept walking and trying to digest what I had seen, I remembered the Beings of Light saying, "Everything is alright, there's nothing to worry about." Feeling free from worry and full of excitement, I repeated those words aloud to my mom. Then I added, "I know that if you dream big you can get big things, Mom!"

"There is much to worry about when there is no food on the table," she scolded. "Look at my oldest brother. He has always been a big dreamer and he has always been hungry. You have to be careful. Dreaming is good, but not to the point that you are out of your own reality."

I knew that I was not simply dreaming because some of my dreams and visions had already manifested, but then I wondered: *Why are some people like my uncle just dreamers who don't succeed? Could I become like him?*

A little later, at the doctor's office, the Beings of Light answered me. "When you dream about something you want you are creating something new, and when you have a vision you are having access to what has already been created, but not yet manifested."

"I know that because you already told me," I interrupted, "but why do some dreams not manifest?" I whispered, holding a magazine.

"Some people never see their dreams manifest because they have been told that such dreams are not possible. Once they limit their mind they deny themselves the possibility to become part of that reality. It will not manifest, or if it does, they will not be aware of it."

"So will all my dreams manifest some day?"

"Yes, they will, but it is best if you don't tell your dreams to everyone. Most people will try to convince you that they are not possible and you could get trapped in that belief."

"Like you said before, we create our own reality!" I exclaimed.

"That's right. You are the result of your own creation. You are what you make of yourself."

"I hope that I can always remember your teaching and never become like my uncle."

"Don't worry, we will be there to remind you. Keep dreaming and creating for yourself, it is all there waiting for you when you are ready."

CHAPTER 13

Protective Forces

I WAS thirteen years old when my mom hired a new maid named Maria. In contrast with the other maids we had before, Maria didn't live in our house. Most of the time the person working at our home was someone that my mom was trying to help. In this case, besides giving Maria a job, my mother had fostered her children, who had lived with us for a while.

Maria had a very hard life and she was holding a lot of anger in her heart. One day when I wouldn't eat the food she was cooking, she got very mad at me and we had an argument. She didn't come back to work for a week, but when she did she said that she needed to ask for my forgiveness.

"It's okay Maria," I responded, "I am also sorry for making you angry the other day. I am glad that you are back."

"It is not that, I really need your forgiveness;" she exclaimed, rubbing her hands nervously.

"What's going on, Maria?" I asked.

"Very few people know this about me," she whispered, "but I practice something called witchery or black magic." Then she fell silent.

Witchcraft was practiced by many Hispanic people across South America and the Caribbean. I had heard stories about people being enchanted, manipulated, and even killed by magical spells.

"Okay Maria, I am listening."

"I was so angry at you the other day that when I went home I tried to cast a spell on you, but things didn't go the way I expected. While I was in the middle of the ritual about a dozen ghost-like entities appeared all around me and shouted: 'You will not hurt this child!' Feeling petrified, I immediately dropped what I was doing and I asked them for forgiveness, and then they disappeared. I couldn't sleep for days and all I could think about was that I needed to ask you for forgiveness. I have practiced black magic for many years and this has never happened to me before."

"Wow!" I exclaimed. More than having any negative feelings, I was amazed about her revelation and curious to know more. After she told me everything I said to her, "I forgive you Maria, but you should know that the more you try to hurt others the more you are hurting yourself and even your family. All the wrong you do to others will come back to you."

"Thank you for forgiving me. I never felt this frightened before."

"Use this as a lesson and stop being angry and trying to hurt people. I know you have had a hard life but you are making it even harder. By the way, I want you to know that black magic cannot hurt me in any way!"

"I am sure of that, Miss Ingrid. After what happened I am never doing this again," she replied, crying as she reached out to hold my hands.

"Let's never talk about this again, okay?" I whispered.

Because I'd heard of black magic, I had once asked the Beings of Light about it. They'd explained that everything was energy, and that people who followed those kinds of practices vibrated in very low energy frequencies.

"Could they hurt me?" I asked.

"People who vibrate in high energy frequencies, like you, cannot be touched by this kind of energy. The frequencies simply don't match like a radio. Your focus of attention is so busy creating that you have the strong tendency to rebuild what others have destroyed. Don't worry or even waste your time thinking about these things."

Feeling reassured, I'd never thought about this matter again until Maria brought it up.

That night after Maria left, I asked the Beings of Light, "You told me once that black magic could not hurt me. If that is true why did you interfere when she was doing the ritual? Could she actually have hurt me?

"It wasn't us, and no, she could not have hurt you."

"What are you saying? Who did it then?"

"The spirits, as you refer to them, that live in the house with you, did it. The mutual awareness and acceptance among all of you have grown so strong that they have become your protectors. You even call one of them by his name."

From the time we moved into the house eleven years prior, we often received phone calls for Mr. Casas. Every time we replied, the person on the phone would go silent and we would just hear static noise. After receiving so many calls we assumed that it was the name of the spirit living in the house, so we started to refer to him as Mr. Casas.

"As we are here to guide you they are here to protect you," the Beings of Light affirmed. Remember last year when one of your cousins was chasing your younger sister around the dinner table, threatening to beat her up?"

"Oh yeah, I remember. How could I forget! It was pretty

creepy when our schoolbooks were lifted in the air by no one and thrown down with great force on the table. That definitely stopped the fight, and my cousin left the house running and screaming in panic. Since then she calls our house the haunted house," I laughed.

"That day they protected your sister from getting hurt. They have done many more things to keep you safe without your knowing."

After what I learned from the Beings of Light I couldn't feel angry at Maria. Instead, I felt incredibly peaceful and grateful. It was so wonderful to discover how many forces there are guiding and protecting us.

CHAPTER 14

Making Peace with My Dad,
Thanks to a Pair of Shoes

WHEN I was young we would get one pair of shoes twice a year, at the start of the new school year and for Christmas. It was Christmas of 1983 when I decided to get a pair of white cloth tennis shoes. My dad was very disappointed with my choice, and selected a pair that he felt was more suitable for a girl. I didn't agree with his decision and remained stubborn, so my dad got very angry at me, and bought the pair that he wanted. I didn't argue anymore, but I was too upset to talk to him for the rest of the day. When we got home he was mad at me for my ungrateful attitude. As a punishment, he took away a tape recorder that he had recently given me for my thirteenth birthday.

At the time I didn't have a strong bond to my dad. I had seen my mom suffering so much because of his work travel and their dysfunctional relationship that I felt little toward him besides resentment and fear. In hindsight, it's no wonder that my parents struggled so much in their marriage, since they were forced to get married when they were only seventeen years old — after my grandparents found out that they had had sex. My parents belonged to very conservative and religious families that could not accept the idea of sex before marriage.

We were also in a patriarchal culture where girls were not supposed to contradict or disrespect men, so it was completely out of the question for me to fight back. Besides, my father had a very strong character, so from a very early age we had learned not to make him angry.

That night with tears in my eyes I asked the Beings of Light for guidance, and they responded to my plea in the most remarkable way.

The following evening right after dinnertime, everyone left the table except my dad and me. I wasn't expecting anything to happen, but once we were alone I sensed the intense presence of the Beings of Light. The space around us became surrounded by their light, accompanied by the delicious fragrance of fresh flowers. At that moment, I felt completely free from any negative feelings towards my dad and a sense of inner peace invaded my entire being. I looked my dad directly in the eyes and words of wisdom started to flow out of my mouth. I didn't know what was happening, but suddenly I found myself talking to him in a way that I had never done before.

"Dad, I will never forget at the age of five, when I told you that I wanted to be a marine scientist when I grew up, your answer was: 'If that is what you want to be then that is what you will be.' That day you made me feel that everything was possible. I know that people do not always get what they want and that makes them very unhappy. I learned that mom and you had to marry when you were very young and that you would rather be free playing drums in a rock band and travelling the world. On another occasion, I overheard you saying that one of your dreams was to become a doctor but since the tuition was too high instead you became a lawyer. Even though you have learned to live with these decisions I know that you are not happy. All these experiences have shown you that there is nothing more compelling in life that getting what you really want, and nothing more disappointing than not getting it. Dad, I know that you want to see me beautiful and I truly appreciate that, but I also want to feel joyful. Things are only things. The real value of a thing is not the thing itself but the meaning that it has for us. Getting what we want is so awesome that it can create everlasting memories. Dad, wouldn't it be amazing that we could surround ourselves only by the things and experiences that we truly desire?"

As more words kept flowing out of my mouth for a while longer, my dad was in complete silence, just staring at me, listening. When I stopped talking he said, "Wait for me here, I will be back." He stood up and walked away towards his bedroom. I was still feeling deeply calm when he came back, bringing the tape recorder. "This belongs to you, I am truly sorry," he stated. At that moment, my entire skin tingled and I felt awed. This was absolutely incredible, considering that his tendency as a lawyer and a man from a macho society was to always fight back.

"Thank you, Dad," I exclaimed.

"Go to bed, it is late," he sighed.

Still feeling grateful while getting ready for bed, I thanked the Beings of Light but I also had a question: "How was I able to talk to my dad in such a way? This has never happened before. I don't think I could have done that without your help."

"Actually, you can. We just helped you ease and quiet your mind so you could communicate with clarity. Talking in such a manner is your natural state of being, you already have done it on many other occasions."

"I guess! But never with my dad," I said.

"As the mind becomes conditioned to a state of fear, it

continuously questions everything that you should or shouldn't do, or feel, or say. This kind of behavior keeps people trapped in loops of judgment and self-doubt. If you learn to quiet your mind, wisdom and clarity will always flow through you. Start by focusing your mind on what feels good, as you did tonight, and the rest will simply unfold."

"Seeing your light and sensing your delicious scent definitely brought me there."

"We are just facilitating, you are the one doing the work. Remember that beyond the limited mind resides the answer to any question. If the conditioned mind is out of the way, situations just get resolved no matter how difficult something seems."

My dad and I didn't say another word about that night anymore, until many years later, but from that day his change was remarkable. We became closer, and shortly afterward my dad started to become interested in my activities. We began engaging in long, deep conversations. He learned how much interest I had in spiritual matters and shared with me some philosophical books written by authors like Plato, Aristotle, and Carl Jung. He also shared stories about his lonely childhood, surrounded by wealth but little affection. His father was a very busy and wealthy businessman who in a jealous rage chased off my father's mother (Grandma Lilia), so my dad grew up with nannies and maids. Learning about his childhood made my heart melt, and the more I perceived him as a little child, the more I could go beyond the negative image I had developed of him.

Curious about these feelings, I asked the Beings of Light what was going on.

"The more you make an effort to understand and unveil any situation, the clearer your mind becomes. With true understanding comes unconditional love, compassion and forgiveness. It is important that you understand that with true love comes spontaneous forgiveness, which doesn't need explanations. It is the forgiveness that comes from knowing that you are here to help each other to evolve, even though sometimes you push each other a little bit too hard."

"The way I feel now is that forgiveness is freedom," I said.

"It is freedom, truly. Remember that the ego is the false idea that you or anyone else is separate from God. When you see everything and everybody as a Whole, you gain clarity, and a clear mind is a free mind; free of judgment."

Talking to my dad brought so much change into our lives. I had never suspected I could experience and understand the meaning of having a close and loving father. Furthermore, we never had to argue again when we shopped, since I was granted the freedom to pick my own shoes.

CHAPTER 15

The Keys of Readiness

I WAS introduced to Transcendental Meditation (TM) thanks to a synchronistic chain of friendships that started with my sister, Lis. TM is a specific form of mantra meditation developed by Maharishi Mahesh Yogi.

While I was attending middle school, a girl from Ecuador moved to Colombia and joined our school. My sister and her became best friends and later she introduced my sister to her brother. Her brother who was attending college became good friends with a guy whose father was the leader of a Transcendental Meditation group. So, by meeting all these people and building close friendships I started practicing group meditation at the age of fourteen. Since I used to be very reserved and rarely opened up to other people, I would only go to meditate. I hardly ever talked to anyone other than the TM leader, or some of the members of my family who also had joined including my dad, grandma and sisters.

As my relationship with my dad grew stronger he also started to try to forgive his mother, Grandma Lilia. My grandmother divorced my grandfather when my dad was only three years old, and not long after, she fled to Venezuela where she remarried and had two more children. So, my dad didn't have the chance to grow up with a mother, a situation that he resented her deeply for.

About a year after we started to practice TM, my grandmother served as a liaison for a spiritual speaker named Jose Garcia to teach a weeklong seminar in Bogota about the developing of spiritual consciousness, the power and opening of the chakras, the Kabbalah, and so on. As a way to reconnect with my grandmother my dad decided to help her with the logistics of this event, helping strengthen their bond. This was the first time I saw my family so connected at a spiritual level.

My dad and I were invited to attend the seminar for free. I felt deeply excited because I had never attended a seminar given by a spiritual speaker. I found his teachings utterly powerful and profound. By now, I had already read many spiritual and philosophical books, so I was able to grasp most of his message. However, my experience of talking about these concepts was minimal, so I felt very shy about approaching him with questions.

The first time I was able to have a little interaction with him was one day during the seminar's lunch break, while eating in a restaurant with the group. "Your Grandma talks a lot about you, she says that you are a very perceptive being," he said, looking at me as I was sitting next to my grandma. He then addressed the group, "Do you know that there are more and more children like her born every year? They are called Indigo children," he stated.

Feeling puzzled, I looked at my grandma. "He is trying to say that you are special," she whispered as he continued explaining the meaning of the Indigo children to everyone. While he was talking I remembered the time when the Beings of Light told me for the first time that I was special.

I was so excited about his comment, not because he referred to me as special, but because this meant there were other children like me in the world. That day I felt that he could guide me more about how to direct my spiritual life. Since he offered private sessions, I asked my grandmother to set up an appointment for me.

Still, I wasn't sure if I was ready for this meeting. As I entered the room and sat in front of him, I felt so nervous that my palms were dripping with sweat and my mouth became as dry as the Sahara. Barely able to talk clearly, I felt so silly that I started off with an apology. Since we only had about twenty minutes to talk due to his busy schedule, I continued by listing all the things that I could perceive, sense, and do since I was little that made me feel so different. I didn't mention the Beings of Light yet, but when he lowered his eyes to look at his watch I felt apprehensive… *Maybe he is way too busy and not that interested about talking with me now… perhaps we can talk another day.*

As I stopped talking we stared at each other and after a short pause he said, "Ingrid, you are a very smart and perceptive child. Just keep reading and studying the way you are doing. There is so much you need to learn, and only time and experience can deliver clear answers to you about the purpose of all your experiences. I would also suggest that you do something to cleanse your system. For example, cleansing your liver will help you reduce any anxiety that you might have and help you be less sensitive to the environment," he said.

At fifteen years of age I couldn't grasp what cleansing my liver had to do with anything. I was looking for some kind of guidance that could help me live a happy life in this world where I felt I didn't belong. I never felt so inadequate before; even though he kept talking for a little longer I couldn't hear him anymore. "Thanks for the advice," I said as the session ended.

Throughout the whole day and into the night, I couldn't stop thinking about how I had been a complete fool, until the Beings of Light said, "Don't beat yourself up. You thought you were not ready and by thinking this way, you clouded your mind with doubt and fear. Nothing clear can come from a clouded mind. On the other hand, you were not the only one feeling apprehensive. He wasn't ready for you either."

"What do you mean?" I asked.

"Most adults underestimate the wisdom of children. There is not much more he could have said to you today."

"I don't understand. He seems so wise. When do you think we are going to be ready?"

"Every single thought is energy, so anything that you have created with your thoughts is energy as well, including your manifested self. For anything more to manifest, you have to be mentally, psychologically and emotionally ready. Only when all the ingredients to make a cake are put together can the cake be baked and then eaten."

"But why do bad moments like today manifest? I wasn't asking for this to happen!" I stated.

"Nothing is bad or good, everything just has different vibrational frequencies. Like a radio, you will be synchronized with the radio station to which you set the dial. Sometimes you may not like what you hear but that doesn't mean it is bad, it only means that you don't resonate with it. The important thing is to know that there are infinite choices, and when you don't resonate with something you always have the power to reset the dial."

"But how can I avoid suffering in the meanwhile?"

"Suffering is not a bad thing, it is just a doorway that can lead you toward what you really want. Sometimes the only way to know if you resonate or not with something is through experience. Knowing what you don't want will always redirect you toward what you want. But it takes time to break old patterns and realign yourself with what you truly desire."

"How do I realign myself?"

"Disconnect from the past and find joy in the now. When you are in a state of joy, the joyful things that you are ready to receive will unfold and manifest."

"These are the type of answers I was looking from Jose. Thank you for being there for me once again. What would I do without you?"

"Every person you meet, everything you learn, every challenge you encounter is there for your own expansion. Never forget that. We are always here for you!"

That day the Beings of Light gave me clarity about not being ready for a spiritual teacher, which freed me from resenting the situation. I also understood that judgment and fear were some of the big obstacles that kept me away from being ready to enjoy other people. Since I was still having these negative feelings, I realized that if I didn't change this mindset, I wasn't going to find the proper ingredients to bake and eat the cake of easy and happy friendships.

CHAPTER 16

Communing with Nature, Including Ticks

A S A teenager, I continued at the same Catholic girls' school I had been in since the sixth grade. Life was easier and happier at home; however, at school things were still very challenging. Since birth I had continuously battled with respiratory problems. I also had a constant fight with food. I was never hungry or thirsty; thus I was always very skinny and due to my appearance people often called me names. But I refused to let my health stop me from being active. I tried to participate in sports and become more social, but was unsuccessful in both pursuits. Even though I had made a couple of friends, we didn't really have much in common. So, I was back to being alone. It seemed that the harder I tried to fit in, the less people liked me.

"Just be yourself," was the advice I got from my grandma Lilia.

"I can be myself at home, Grandma, but no one at school likes me the way I am. I even heard rumors that some kids were afraid of me. They say that I am too odd." At this point in my life, it was completely clear to me that I wasn't like anyone else I knew, not even like my grandmother. "Why do I have to be so different from everyone else?" This was my ongoing question, no matter how many times I heard that my uniqueness was a gift.

In my sophomore year, our religion teacher decided that we would play a group game. The game consisted of assigning an animal to each person that seemed to fit her personality. During the game, each person would sit on a chair in the middle of the classroom while the rest of the class would take a few minutes to discuss which animal. Then someone would announce the animal, and explain the group's choice. People were assigned different animals, from dolphins, to eagles, to horses, even a unicorn. When my turn came, I was anxious to hear what they had to say about me. I always felt that I wanted to be a bird. *If I could just grow wings I could fly anywhere I wanted and I would be free.* That's what I was thinking while the rest of the class was debating.

There was a lot of commotion in the room until the teacher yelled, "Everyone please silence." Then my heart sank very deep into my chest when one of the popular girls murmured, "A tick."

"Excuse me?" the teacher said sternly.

"A tick," the girl reaffirmed. Some of the girls burst into laughter while others remained silent.

"Everybody quiet," the teacher demanded. "Why is she a tick?"

"Because she is annoying and hard to get rid of."

At that moment, the school bell rang and everyone except two girls and the teacher left the classroom. I felt so sad and humiliated. "We do not agree with them," one of the two girls said to me, "That was mean and childish." From that day Luisa and Monica walked away from their own groups, and we became friends.

Amazingly, only a couple of weeks before the animal game, I had decided to follow grandma's advice: Stop trying to make friends by doing things I didn't like, including playing sports. Since I did like to play chess I joined the chess team, which only had a few members, one of whom was Luisa. I remember thinking how much I enjoyed chatting with her while playing chess.

While talking to the Beings of Light about the class incident and my new friends, they made me laugh by saying, "Ticks are also part of God."

"I know, but you are being silly," I replied.

"Thanks to that tick you have gained two new friends."

"You couldn't be more right," I laughed.

To my surprise, only two weeks later I also made another friend named Thomas. Since I had shown a strong interest in becoming a marine biologist, our principal asked me if I wanted to meet her nephew, who was working with the Colombian National Park Service in that field. I was very excited to meet him. He was about fifteen years older than me, but from the moment we met we connected and became very good friends.

"Wow, I didn't know I was ready to meet all these new people," I said to the Beings of Light.

"To be ready you don't need to make any huge effort. As we told you before, the more you focus on the positive, as you have been doing at home and lately at school, the more you make yourself ready to meet your dreams," they replied.

Thomas happened to be a very wise and a sensitive person and he taught me much of what I learned about metaphysics. My friendship with Thomas, Monica and Luisa grew and remained strong throughout the rest of my high school years.

* * *

When I was sixteen, we were finally able to move from our haunted house to a new one located near a big beautiful park. Going from an urban to a suburban environment was so dramatic that being at this new place felt like a dream. By now I had developed such a profound love for nature that I would spend hours at the park meditating, exercising and contemplating everything in nature.

About six months after the move, one Saturday morning I went to the park by myself. It was a warm and a very quiet day. After exercising on the monkey bars, I sat on top and closed my eyes to enjoy the warm breeze and listen to the birds. Afterwards I walked on a pathway toward a grassy area nearby. As my approaching foot was about to touch the grass, I heard a very loud sound coming from the ground. Surprised, I moved back. When I stepped forward again, the sound repeated and I thought, *Could this possibly be coming from the grass?* So, instead of stepping on it I went down on my knees and slowly approached it with my hand. Every time I touched the grass it produced this loud, pleasant sound. Astonished I asked the Beings of Light, "What is this?"

"The grass is welcoming you," I heard. "It loves when people sit or lay on it," they added.

I immediate dove onto it. "Wow! It sure sounds and feels wonderful! I guess that's why people usually enjoy sitting on the grass so much, without even knowing it is welcoming us."

"Indeed," they answered.

I felt deeply excited because this was absolutely amazing. It was a beautiful piece of classical music. I wondered how it was possible that I couldn't hear such a distinct sound before. "When you are profoundly connected with nature you can hear what is beyond your ears," the Beings of Light whispered.

"My mom and grandma aren't going to believe this one," I laughed.

After that, going to the park and sitting on the grass became my favorite thing to do. I could not always hear its sounds, but I could always sense how alive it was. Not long after, I also started to hear the plants that were living in my house, especially the one sitting in the living room that my mom had had for years. It was her favorite.

One morning as my mom was watering and talking to her plant, I told her what had happened in the park. "Plants are very sensitive, they love to be touched and pampered," she responded. "I cannot hear them, but I can sense their aliveness. You are a very perceptive person so it doesn't surprise me that you could sense something like that." At that moment the plant made a sudden movement and a sound. Astonished, my mom who was kneeling in front of the plant fell backwards on the floor and started to laugh. "Oh! My God this is incredible," she yelled.

After that it kept happening to us often. It was always a deeply emotional experience, because making a connection like this was something that simply blew our minds.

About a year later after the event happened with the grass, my friend Thomas introduced me to the teachings of an English surgeon named Dr. Edward Bach, founder of flower essence therapy. Dr. Bach was a pioneer in understanding the connection of our emotional bodies to our physical health. He developed flower remedies, known as Bach Healing Herbs, to treat the underlying emotional causes of diseases.

Thomas had been using the remedies for years, and invited me to a three-day training course that focused on remedy knowledge and developing awareness. During the second day of training, one of the exercises was to sit in front of a bunch of different plants and try to sense the medicinal purposes of each one. The plants were aligned in a row with no name. So, without an identifier I sketched them in a notebook and assigned each a number. As I closed my eyes and focused on my breathing, I started to sense the energy of the plants. I felt very peaceful and deeply connected. Throughout the exercise, barely opening my eyes, I wrote for each number what I sensed from the plants and at the end I showed my answers to Thomas.

When the instructor revealed the medicinal purpose of each plant, we were speechless as we discovered that I had written the exact answers. I really wasn't expecting this to happen; I didn't feel like I had any special powers. Feeling very excited, Thomas wanted to tell the others, but I didn't want him to do so. He knew that I was very reserved so he respected my decision. He was using the healing herbs for himself and to help others. After the training he wanted me to do the same, but I wasn't really interested. At the time, I was still pretty much a loner and other than sharing my mystical experiences with my family, I didn't feel like opening myself to anyone else.

After taking the class my connection with nature, which kept growing stronger, also brought me to feel more in touch with my own body. Sitting at the park in meditation and being able to hear the birds, to sense the breeze, to feel the warmth of the sun touching my skin or the rain bathing my body, I realized that I often didn't realize that I had this body, unless I was tired or feeling pain. I finally understood what my grandmother meant when she said that the body was a temple that could be used as a doorway to achieve inner peace.

At the time, I didn't use the gift of communicating with plants for making remedies, but I learned and started to teach others the importance of respecting nature. I couldn't even cut a flower without asking it first for permission. Being one with nature is like expanding ourselves beyond the limits of anything we could ever have imagined. By connecting with nature I felt connected with God.

CHAPTER 17

Going Deeper Into the Teachings

ABOUT a year after Jose Garcia came to Colombia from Puerto Rico to teach his first seminar, he returned to teach a second one. Jose received so much support in Colombia that he decided he would return for the third time less than a year later. However, the situation in Colombia with the drug cartels became so difficult that it was not safe for a US citizen to be in our country.

To find the way to continue his teachings seven people including Grandma, Dad and I became part of a group called Agni Yoga. Agni means fire in Sanskrit — the Creative Fire of the Universe. I was the youngest of the group at sixteen.

In the group no one was considered the leader, but we were following the guidance of a highly educated person with a degree in medicine, Dr. Mario Chavez, who had been studying and practicing the Hindu ancient philosophy known as Vedanta for years. He was also following the teachings of Master Morya, an Ascended Master and the guru of Helena Blavatsky, a founder of the Theosophical Society.

Every Saturday evening we would gather at the house of one of the members to study and discuss some very profound teachings coming from books like the *Leaves of Morya's Garden I (The*

Call) and *II (Illumination),* the *Crest Jewel of Discrimination* or *Vivekachudamani* (in Sanskrit) that I already had been reading for a few years, *Self-Realization* or *Aparokshanubhuti* (in Sanskrit), and the *Bhagavad Gita*, also known as *The Song of the Bhagavan* (Guru or God).

After learning about the existence of illuminated beings known as Ascended Masters I asked the Beings of Light, "Are any of you what we would call an Ascended Master?"

"In essence we are all the same. We all belong to the same universal consciousness as a Whole, but some of us have different levels of evolution and expansion."

"How is that?"

"Experience," they answered; "the more you experience, the more you evolve and expand. So yes, some of us are what you call Ascended Masters. You also wonder why you see us with different colors, don't you?"

"Yes I do! You know that I am just starting to read a book that my friend Thomas gave me, that talks about colors meaning different things."

"Again, we are all the same, but depending on our level of evolution we have different vibrational frequencies. This is the reason why you see us projecting different colors. When we appear to you, the color that you see matches not just your vibrational frequency at the moment, but also the situation as a whole."

"The color that I see most often is blue," I said excitedly.

"How does this color make you feel?"

"It makes me feel very safe and secure. It takes my fears away and gives me the courage to resolve any situation. But why do I rarely see Beings with other colors?"

"All of us are always here for you, but you are only aware of us when you bring yourself to a high vibration. The more elevated you are, the more access you have to highly evolved beings."

"My guess is that the silver ones are probably much more evolved because I have rarely ever seen them. How do I get myself to vibrate higher?"

"Love. Pure unconditional Love is the highest vibrational energy there is."

"It is not always easy to feel that kind of love," I huffed.

"Appreciation and gratitude can also bring you there, because you only appreciate what makes you feel great. The better you feel, the more connected you are with us."

At the time it became evident to me that the higher I kept myself vibrating, the clearer and easier it was to make decisions and to take the right actions. One of those good decisions happened about a year after I became part of the Agni Yoga. One day Dr. Chavez talked about a group called Maiz (Corn). The name was given because of the sacred meaning that corn has to many Indian cultures in the Americas. He said that he was truly impressed with the amount of knowledge that the leader of this group, Herman Rodríguez, had about the Indians. I always wanted to know more about the Indian cultures because of their deep connection to nature.

I was seventeen when I went to Herman's house where they held the Maiz meetings. When I knocked on the door I was invited to come in by Herman himself. I was the first one arriving that evening, so I introduced myself and we had time to chat for a while. I told him about Agni Yoga, TM, and some of the teachings that I had been receiving, and the more he listened the more interested he was in me. That day I felt so welcomed by him and the rest of the members of the group that I decided to also join Maiz.

Herman was indeed a very wise and spiritual person. He had

been practicing Hinduism and had been surrounded by enlightened people such as Paramahamsa Niranjan since he was a little child. Niranjan came from India and spent a few years living in Herman's house when they were growing up. Herman also spent a few years living in an ashram, and now he was dedicated to the study of astrology and to digging deep into the roots of various philosophies and cultures.

The meetings in Maiz were absolutely beautiful. The room was very cozy and everybody sat on the floor in a circle. Herman would read a passage from different sacred Indian scriptures, like the *Popol Vuh* (Book of the People), and a "talking stick" was passed around the room, giving every person the chance to speak. As the stick was passed from one person to the other, they looked each other in the eyes, and with one hand placed over the heart, one person would say, "*In Lak'esh*" while the other replied, "*Ala K'in*" — which in Mayan means "I am you," and "You are me."

We also used these words every time we met someone or at the time to leave Maiz. I loved doing this so much that I started to repeat in my mind "*In Lak'esh*" to every person I met.

Over time, a strong feeling of love for humanity began to evolve within me, which was confusing at first because I was still apprehensive about talking and being with people. Thankfully, the Beings of Light gave me relief when they said, "To share love you don't need to say a word, you only have to be present. The same way you share your love with nature, you can do with people. There is no need to separate the two. And when you are ready to talk, the words will come."

By now, at seventeen, I was deeply immersed in spirituality. I continued reading and actively participating in the activities within Maiz, the Agni Yoga and TM while I was also practicing meditation at home. Additionally, I had learned more than a dozen mantras written in Sanskrit and Latin that I chanted every day. I deeply resonated with all these teachings, because for the first time I was starting to grasp the link between a secular and a spiritual life.

* * *

A few months after joining Maiz, I participated in a weekend retreat that began on a Friday evening with a dancing and cleansing ceremony at Herman's house, guided by a very old shaman named Master Cirilo. It was amazing to see this man, who appeared older than all of us combined together, dancing and singing with so much energy and passion, giving us the drive to enjoy the dance until around midnight.

This first day was followed by an early start on Saturday. All of us sat in a warm and dark room, illuminated only by a little candle. I loved this type of enclosed and cozy environment, where I felt extremely comfortable. Throughout the day Herman taught us a few sacred Mayan mantras and their meanings.

"*Hun Ol*," he chanted out loud, making my body tremble. "United together as one heart, one mind, one intention, one will; together as the fingers attached to the hand, with harmony and peace. Although we are all different on the exterior we belong to the same source, hearts beating all together as one," he explained.

Oh My God! I thought. *This is what the Beings of Light meant when they said that we are one essence — one hand, but each one of us, the fingers, is different. It is our uniqueness that encompasses unity.*

After talking for a while and repeating this mantra a few times, he chanted the next: "*Chi'kol T'anit'an*," which signifies listen attentively and speak only the truth, and "*Etaili*," meaning fraternity, grace and friendship. These were followed by "*Hal Ol*." Then he said, "Trust — it signifies the deep trust or faith that we should have in divine guidance, or what we call God."

Oh God! At that moment I remembered: "Trust us when we say that everything is alright." Those were the words I had been hearing from the Beings of Light since I was little.

Once again, after explaining the meaning of these mantras and leading us in a chant, he offered the last one: *"K'uchpaha'n Yo'ol."* After a deep breath he said, "Determination, patience and constancy. It is the one who overcomes any obstacle to reach his goal. It is the one who does not fear failure. The only thing that stops us from succeeding is the fear of failing; once this obstacle is removed we can become free to move forward in any direction. But this can be done only when we trust, when we have faith in God."

I recalled how amazingly well I felt when I left my body during my NDE, and sensed the presence of the Beings of Light for the first time. I felt so deeply touched by these mantras. It was as if they were being chanted by the Beings of Light. To me they summarized the core of their teachings.

On Sunday, we continued the last day of the weekend retreat in a country house located in the middle of a beautiful valley surrounded by mountains. There, twenty people and I witnessed Master Cirilo performing the most powerful ritual I had ever seen.

At noon he wanted to do a healing ceremony outdoors using incense and fire. From the time we arrived early in the morning it was pouring rain, so we stayed indoors for a couple of hours chatting and drinking hot chocolate while we waited for the weather to clear up.

While everyone was starting to worry about postponing the ceremony or doing it indoors, Master Cirilo didn't seem concerned at all. "Don't worry, everything is alright," he kept repeating. It was still pouring when he said, "Let's go, it is time to start."

"First, let's grab some umbrellas," someone yelled.

"It is not needed," he calmly answered.

We thought that maybe he didn't mind that we all got wet. However, as we walked outside with him and stood around in a circle, not a drop of rain touched us. Before we left the house Master Cirilo had started to chant some mantras in a native Indian language. He was holding in his hands burning leaves and incense, swirling around in the air. He was so focused on his ritual that his face looked as if he was in a trance. As he chanted, the clouds above us started to open, allowing the most beautiful sunrays to come through. We were all in complete awe while he did his ceremony.

As we kept murmuring in disbelief because it kept raining except where we were standing, he chanted to the elements, now in Spanish, and kept doing his rituals until he had cleansed every one of us with his sage, incense, and mantras. When he finished his healing ceremony we all went indoors. The clouds came back and the rain kept falling throughout the rest of the day. As everyone asked questions he simply answered, "It is Mother Nature's will."

"But how is this possible?" someone asked.

"When you are one with nature everything is possible," he said quietly.

Seeing him perform this "miracle" was in itself amazing, but what amazed me the most was that he remained absolutely humble. I couldn't stop thinking, *God, if there is anything I need to learn today it is how to become as humble as this holy man.* He remains one of the most humble yet powerful people I have ever had the privilege to meet.

At this time of my life after receiving so many powerful teachings and messages of unity, not just by the Beings of Light but also by Master Cirilo, Herman Rodriguez, Jose Garcia, Grandma Lilia, the Agni Yoga and TM, I realized that the concept of oneness held the same valid truth throughout the whole spectrum of cultures and religions including Christianity. The only differences were the ways in which the story was being told.

"A mountain has only one summit. But the mountain is so giving that it has allowed more than a million paths to be carved around it for everyone to reach its summit," the Beings of Light explained to me.

"So, there are no chosen ones?" I asked.

"You chose yourself. It is up to you to pick or to create a new path, to walk the path, and to reach the summit."

"Will I get there?"

"You will, if you choose to do so."

CHAPTER 18

Faith & Determination

WHEN I was in my senior year of high school, my parents fell into a very difficult financial situation that brought us to the verge of losing everything we had. My mom, an extremely strong woman who had conquered numerous obstacles in her life, one day reached her deepest point of despair. I was talking with her in her bedroom early in the afternoon when she looked at me and shouted, "If by seven o'clock tonight your dad doesn't come home with the money we need to solve this dreadful situation, I will stop believing in God."

My dad had been suspended from work and was under investigation due to some work-related issues. He had been confined for months in the headquarters of the Security Service Agency of Columbia, where he was working at the time, and he was to remain there until his case was resolved.

Feeling deeply sad and filled with anguish after hearing these words coming from my mom, who truly believed in God, I looked at her and said, "Mom, I have seen the impossible happen, like rain being stopped by a shaman. Maybe this time God will also put a stop to what is happening to Dad."

"I don't know, but this is my last call to God for help," she repeated.

This is going to be a very hard one for God to resolve, I had to admit to myself. *I don't see how my dad could be home tonight.* I felt lost and sorrowful.

At that very moment, a beam of light coming from a picture of the Sacred Heart of Jesus that was hanging from her bedroom wall bathed my mom's entire chest. When I saw it I yelled, "Mom, look at the light."

My mom who was sitting on the bed saw the light and yelled, "Oh my God what is this, what is happening?"

As she put her hand on her chest the light faded away. I was sitting next to her holding on tight to her other hand in complete awe, as we both cried deeply.

"This too is going to be resolved," she sobbed.

"I am sure of that Mom, this is a sign from God. Dad might not come tonight but everything will be alright."

Throughout the rest of the day I thought about the Beings of Light while praying to them for help.

That very night a miracle, bigger than Master Cirilo making the rain stop, happened. At seven o'clock my dad came back home and he was carrying with him the money we needed to pay all our debts. He also gave us the amazing news of his return to work. That very day he'd been told he was cleared of all charges and was free to go home. As it turned out, the people at his office had already created a fund to help compensate my dad for the money he had lost.

My dad gave us the biggest surprise of our lives, arriving unannounced that night. For my mom and myself it wasn't just a surprise; it was a way to undoubtedly know that faith in God can definitely move mountains.

* * *

My friendship with Monica and Luisa continued all the way through our senior year. At the point when everyone else was anxiously thinking about the state testing for college, Luisa and I were preoccupied with a completely different issue. We had decided not to be part of a very important religious ceremony, the Sacrament of Confirmation, that happened at our school every year before graduation. At the time, more than 95 % of the population in Colombia was Catholic and everybody we knew followed the dogma and rituals without doubt or complaints. Not us! Despite the possibility of getting in trouble and perhaps not being able to graduate, we refused to participate.

Luisa and I had different reasons. Luisa considered herself an agnostic and I had given up the idea of following any beliefs that involved fearing God, or the idea that I was a sinner. When I nearly died I had experienced myself as a Being of Light shining pure and innocent, engulfed in an atmosphere of absolute love and joy. That was the God I knew. To me it was amazing to know that I didn't have to fear the *One* who loved me the most.

When I told my parents about my decision they were hesitant because they were worried I couldn't gradate, but then I asked them, "If God is absolute compassion and universal forgiveness, how could I be a sinner in the eyes of God? Am I a sinner to God? Or am I a sinner only to people who believe in sin? Mom, Dad, I cannot go with something I don't believe." Since my parents were involved in all my spiritual activities they knew that they couldn't force me to do it.

"Okay, we will talk to the school principal," they answered.

As a good lawyer my dad got me out of it, and I was able to graduate with all my senior classmates. For the first time in my life

I felt so empowered because I was able to keep my position despite knowing that most everyone might oppose my decision and judge me. Having my friends and parents support me was all that mattered.

Now that I graduated, it was time to think about college. In Colombia, there was no question about going to college; otherwise you were no one, a person with no future. Fortunately, when I finished high school, I was one of the few that knew for sure what I wanted to do and had the full support of my parents. Choosing the school was a no brainer since at the time there was only one college in Colombia offering a program of study about the marine environment.

My love for the ocean started when my parents brought me to see it for the very first time at the age of four. That day, the minute I walked on the sand and saw the vast ocean I was completely absorbed by it. I put my feet into the water and stared at it until I heard my mom calling me, "Ingrid, Ingrid! Are you okay?" I turned and said to my mom, "It looks like a blanket that goes forever. Mom, someday I will find what is hidden under it!"

At only four, I didn't know I was having one of my first visions. After that trip happened I was lured in by any book or picture that was related to the ocean. I just wanted to know what was underneath that blanket. I learned that the ocean was teeming with life, and that it was possible to study it because one of my uncles had gone to college to study Marine Science.

One day at the age of five, I approached my dad who was leaning on the patio door while smoking a cigarette, and I said to him, "When I grow up I am going to become a marine scientist, just like my Uncle Alvaro."

My dad looked at me and said, "Okay, if that is what you want to do, that is what you will do."

Years later, I was accepted into the program and started my career as a Marine Biologist. Some people told me that with this career I would not be able to find jobs or make much money. At eighteen I had many uncertainties about the future like everyone else, but nothing anyone said bothered me because I was clear about succeeding. As the Beings of Light told me, "To reach the summit the only thing you need is your will."

CHAPTER 19

The Light at the End of the Street

O N MY WAY one night to practice Transcendental Meditation with the group, the bus had to drop me off three
blocks farther than my usual stop due to a detour caused by
a car accident. Usually, I would have had to walk about five blocks
from the bus stop to the house beside a large busy avenue, but this
time I had to take a different route. The street was quite dark and
deserted, but I didn't think much about it and started to walk.
After four blocks I began to feel as if someone was watching me,
so I started to walk faster. Then, suddenly somebody was right
behind me wrapping my upper body with his arm, while another
person jumped in front of me with a knife.

Both men were dressed in black. I was wearing a black leather
jacket they wanted, besides my money. I felt an intense fear piercing
my entire being, then I immediately thought, *Beings of Light, help
me!* At that very moment I was able to see that the aura of the guy
threatening me with the knife was very dim, colored with blotches
of grey and red. I lowered my eyes and saw that the arms of the guy
holding me had a similar aura. Then, I sensed they too were in fear.
However, in contrast to them, my aura was still shining bright.
Right then I became remarkably calm and totally fearless. Feeling
empowered I looked at the guy with the knife and said, "Well if

you want my jacket, then your friend needs to let go of my arms."

As soon as my arms were freed, I leaned a little bit forward and with all my strength, swung my right elbow backwards, hitting the man behind me directly in the groin. I knew exactly where to hit him because I had felt his body when he was standing behind me. I was a small and skinny girl, but I must have hit him pretty fiercely because he yelled in agony. As he moved backwards and bent his body due to the pain I crouched and turned to the left, to avoid the man with the knife standing in front of me.

"Run back towards the bus stop," I heard the Beings of Light say.

Although I was closer to my destination than the bus stop, I did what I was instructed to do. I could have given the thieves my jacket and the little money I had, but I loved that jacket. It had been given to me by an uncle who was now deceased. Besides, I sensed that the assailants were going to cause me further harm.

Everything happened so fast and unexpectedly that it took a few seconds for the two men to react. By now I'd gained the advantage of surprise, and they seemed clueless about what to do. I ran so fast! I almost felt as if I was being lifted and pushed forward. At the very end of the street I saw a bright light, so I headed toward it.

At this point the two guys were running behind me yelling all kinds of obscenities. When I was able to reach the light I realized that it came from a shop and as I flung the door open I saw a security guard standing right inside. I entered the shop yelling, "I am being followed by two men who are trying to rob me!" The men stopped, looking at us from a distance and then fled.

When I realized I was free from danger, my body shook uncontrollably and I wet my pants. By then the guard and two other people were surrounding me. Looking down at my pants I said,

"I am sorry, could I please use the phone to call my father?"

An older man who identified himself as the shop owner patted me on the back and guided me to the phone desk, where I was able to talk to my dad. The place turned out to be a barbershop and the security guard happened to be their last customer. While waiting for my dad, the owner said, "Oh dear, you are so lucky, by this time we are usually closed." Pointing at the guard he added, "Mr. Jose might have saved your life tonight."

Still shaking, I looked at Mr. Jose and as a lady gave me a glass of water the owner continued saying, "The only reason we are still open is because Mr. Jose arrived late asking for a haircut and we agreed because we knew him."

That night, the guard was just leaving the barbershop as I ran in.

My dad, also on his way to the TM meeting picked me up, thanked the barber, and brought me home. That night while talking to the Beings of Light I felt so thankful for their protection and guidance. Since I had never been in a situation like this before I was curious to know how was I able to go from extreme fear to complete calm at the moment of the attack.

"Fear and stress are the body and mind's first line of defense. If you use them as they are, warnings, they can work to your advantage. For example, if someone was born without the possibility of feeling physical pain and got appendicitis, then their appendix would burst and kill them without warning. Feelings of pain, fear, and stress force you to make choices, and by making new choices you grow and expand. The question is how long you will take to make your choices."

"Oh, I got it. The longer you take to choose, the more miserable you will become, turning yourself into a fearful person."

"Yes, that's the kind of fear that makes you think that you are alone and disempowered. It's not useful."

"I see, like the two robbers! That's why their auras were so dimmed."

"That's right."

"So why did I feel so empowered?"

"Fear can make your adrenaline surge. Using that to your advantage can help you focus. Since you already knew that we are here with you, you were ready to listen and follow our guidance."

"Having you with me is a treasure."

"We are with everyone that calls for us. However, we are not here to stop certain experiences from happening. If you call for us and learn to attune yourself with us, like you have done, we can always guide you."

"Why did I go back to feeling so fearful once I was inside the shop?"

"That is the physiological response of your body after a very stressful situation. It needs to go back to balance. At that moment you just let yourself be and release all those feelings. The important thing is not to stay attached to the experience and create a big drama. Suffering comes when you think that something bad has happened to you, and you are not able to let go. Look at the experience as a whole and you will find the purpose behind any experience. Suffering is a matter of choice. If you are able to remain present, there is no need to attach yourself to a traumatic story. Always remember that whatever happened is not happening anymore. Just let go of the past and be grateful for the now."

At this age how could I have ever known that by almost being brutally robbed, I was going to learn one of the most important lessons of my life? Stress and fear, if clearly understood, could actually be used to my advantage!

CHAPTER 20

The Island

BEFORE I started college in 1989 at the age of eighteen, I decided that I wanted to make a big change in my life, and become more open. I wanted to leave behind the shy, solitary person I was during my school years. With determination, I made it happen, becoming more popular and meeting many people from the very beginning of college.

Although I was able to change my personality on the surface, I was still feeling apprehensive about interacting with people on a deeper level. The real challenge was not about approaching others, but feeling that I could belong in their world. Many times I wanted to run and hide in the world of the Beings of Light, far away from the eyes of the human world. I thought perhaps it was not possible for a girl like me to find complete happiness in this world.

In an effort to try new experiences, during my first summer break of college I volunteered for six weeks to serve as a Park Ranger in a program offered by the National Park Service of Colombia. With a new friend, Mariana, I applied to go to a remote island called Gorgona, a few miles off the Pacific Coast of Colombia.

This experience turned out to be an amazing adventure from the start, beginning with the road trip to the west coast to catch any commercial boat that would take us to the island. We boarded one that was carrying timber.

Gorgona was a protected sanctuary, so apart from the staff no more than ten visitors were allowed on the island at any given time, and visitors could stay for a maximum of five days. Since they wanted to restrict human influence on the area, the space for housing was very limited and most of the facilities were very rustic. Apart from two computers assigned to the scientist and a couple of radios, there were no other electronics. Since electricity was run by a generator there was only a few hours of electric power available during the day. At night we only used lamps and candles making the place appear very mysterious.

This isolated island was also a tropical forest, packed with insects, poisonous snakes, venomous spiders and many other exotic and dangerous creatures. Once there, my friend and I realized that two urban girls would have many challenges to face together.

The first day on the island we were in training about the dangers and wonders of this place, learning what we were allowed to do and not to do. We were assigned different duties and responsibilities. Part of my work was to serve as a tour guide for the visitors, but my most important assignment was to assist the chief scientist with whatever she needed for her research projects. Besides these obligations, I was also assigned to collect information from the weather station on the island. So every day around seven in the morning I would walk by myself for about twenty minutes to the station to read and log the information in the logbook. Then I would take a few more minutes to meditate and another twenty minutes to come back to the settlement.

I really liked that my assignments gave me the opportunity to balance the time I was required to share with other people and the time that I needed to be on my own. I didn't find it easy to live in a small community where we all knew everybody's whereabouts. After less than a week I discovered that even in a small community like this, there was space for immense drama between people. I always detested such drama, and finding it unavoidable even in this remote piece of the world made me think that maybe it wasn't worth it to try belonging in this world.

Around the end of the second week on the island I was feeling kind of low in energy and motivation. One morning after collecting the weather data, I decided to walk a little further until I found a hill where the views of the surrounding area were absolutely breathtaking. It felt so calming that I decided to sit and devote some time to deep meditation. While sensing the presence of the Beings of Light, I usually could bring myself mentally to a place where I could feel less touched by reality.

"What am I doing on this stupid island?" I asked the Beings of Light.

At the end of the meditation, as I opened my eyes, I felt as if I were the epicenter of the universe. In deep amazement, I felt that I could perceive everything happening around me, in multiple directions at the same time. My senses became very sharp, allowing me to hear every sound, to sense every smell, to see the intensity of every color and to perceive beauty and harmony in all aspects of this reality. Everything was happening at once and everything was in constant motion — then suddenly, it stopped. Everything became still and silent. It was then that I was able to sense for the very first time, with my eyes open, that it was possible to achieve unity with the Whole while carrying a human body. I didn't need to die or to be out of this body; I could achieve oneness with whatever I was, here and now.

At that moment, a profound spiritual teaching came into my

mind: "When you think that you are too much, remember that you are but a speck of dust in the vast universe. And, when you feel like you are nothing, remember that you are as whole as the universe." I remembered the feelings of awe I experienced when I saw a bacterial cell under a microscope for the first time. I realized that in the eyes of the universe I was in fact a speck of dust, but in the eyes of a microorganism I would be a universe. Seeing entire communities of microorganisms teeming with life in one single drop of seawater brought me to recognize the vastness of this universe.

The feelings of peace, tranquility and unity that I experienced that day on the island were so deep that I was able to realize that it was possible to feel real joy while living in the human dream.

We spent only six weeks on the island, but it felt as if we had been there for a year. All that was bothersome at the beginning turned into the most fulfilling experiences of my life. Being able to experience oneness at this level enabled me to take the first steps toward understanding that I was free to choose the way in which I wanted to perceive my own reality. After that I was able to switch my mood, from being down and complaining about my reality, to appreciating every moment as it was given to me on the island. Not having to care about time, or possessions, or trends, or traffic, or any of the stresses associated with living in a big city became priceless to me. Being able to sit on the beach at night, admiring the beauty of the stars, watching dolphins jumping on the horizon while carrying with them the light produced by bioluminescent plankton, and listening to the noises of the jungle, I realized that I was in a world of wonders —but only if I chose to see it that way.

Every five days I had the chance to meet new people visiting the island, and guide them through all the adventures that a place like this could offer. By listening to people and observing their behavior,

I discovered that an extreme environment like this was the perfect opportunity to test my endurance and see my true nature. For some people, spending more than a week in an isolated place like this would be torture, but for others, heaven. This was indeed a world of contrasts. Every day I spent on this island I was able to see more deeply that being different as I was could truly be a gift.

CHAPTER 21

Three Faces, One Heart

A T THE end of my first year of college, during the Christmas holiday of 1989, two college friends and I decided to go on a month long trip to Ecuador. I had met Gunter and Fernando after my trip to Gorgona Island, and introduced them to the group Maiz, where we all learned a great deal about the inner workings and rituals of the Indian cultures of the Americas. Gunter's family lived in Quito, Ecuador and he wanted to show us the beauties of his country, including Inca temples located in the Andes.

During our trip we visited many amazing cities and small villages in the Andean mountains, and along the Pacific Coast. The most amazing experience of the entire journey happened when we visited an ancient pre-Inca temple located in the Andes, in the province of Cañar. This temple known as Ingapirca is the largest known Inca ruin in Ecuador.

The day we arrived in the area, on the way to the temple we first stopped at the home of an Indian family who offered us some hot beverages, since it was very early in the morning and chilly. Their home was very small and humble, and even though they didn't seem to have many possessions they all looked happy. To express our gratitude we gave them a little money and then continued on our way to the temple.

Before entering the complex we practiced an Indian ritual, in which one asks the spirits guarding the temple for permission to cross the threshold. During the ritual we evoked the mystical forces that govern the four main cardinal directions. Then we asked each one for permission to enter, offering our gratitude to them and all divine forces for allowing us to be there. When we started the ritual, there was no wind blowing, but as we were performing the ritual a wind with a low whistling sound started to grow around us.

We had our eyes closed but as the wind kept increasing in intensity we opened our eyes and smiled at each other, tightly holding hands.

"I think that we are being welcomed by the guardians of the Temple," Fernando said with a smile.

As we finished the ritual the wind calmed down and then remained still for the rest of the day. Feeling very excited while entering the temple, we kept talking about what had just happened, sensing that we were surrounded by the mystical forces that we had evoked. I already knew that it was possible to communicate with the world of the elements because not long before I had witnessed the shaman, Master Cirilo, stop the rain.

As we walked for a while together through the temple, Gunter explained to us some of the architectural details of this intricate ancient structure. He reported that the Incas called it the "temple of the sun" because it was positioned so that on the solstices, at exactly the right time of day, sunlight would fall through the center of the portal located in the small chamber at the top of the temple.

Before leaving the temple, we decided to split up so everyone could have some time alone. I felt free to sit wherever I wanted and dedicate a few minutes to meditating in peace. After thanking God and the Beings of Light for this new experience, I continued walking around and enjoying the day and the views.

After wandering for a while, I suddenly had the feeling that someone was looking at me. When I turned around I saw my friends far off in the distance, minding their own business. Then I thought I saw something moving fast on the ground, but what I thought might have been an animal surprised me.

A small rock resembling a face was lying on the ground right next to my feet, positioned in a way that gave the impression that it was looking at me. When I picked it up and held it in my hand, I sensed a vibrating energy. Overjoyed with emotion I looked at the sky, thanking again the Beings of Light. I kissed the stone and held it tight in my hand as I ran to show this treasure to my friends.

As I approached Gunter he said, "I have something extra-ordinary to tell you. I was sitting right here on the ground with my eyes closed when I had the feeling of someone staring at me. When I opened my eyes I found this lying on the ground right in front of me."

As he was talking he opened his hand and revealed a rock with the shape of a face, very similar to the one that I just had found. Then I jumped in excitement and showed him what I was holding in my hand.

"No way, how is this possible?" he exclaimed.

At that moment Fernando was walking toward us and asked what was happening. We opened our hands and showed him the rocks. He looked at us, shocked, as he pulled from his pocket a third rock. He also said that he had the feeling of being observed, and after looking around he guided his eyes to the ground and found the rock right on his path. Then Gunter said, "The fact that this happened almost simultaneously to two of us seems almost impossible, but to the three of us! That's what I consider a miracle."

To prove if this indeed was a miracle, we walked all around the perimeter looking for more rocks with a similar shape. After looking for more than an hour, we couldn't find anything remotely close in appearance. Then we sat in a circle and gathered the three rocks on Gunter's bandanna, so we could admire them all together. Then we found something else even more remarkable about the rocks.

They were all similar in appearance since they all looked like a face, but they had different sizes and colors. The biggest one was reddish orange, the medium one was grey, and the smallest one was white. Gunter who was the tallest and had bright red hair had found the red rock, Fernando who was the darkest of the three of us with deep black hair had found the grey rock, and I, being the smallest and lightest in skin tone, had found the white one. This was beyond coincidental. We held each other's hands and offered a prayer of gratitude to God and all the holy forces surrounding us. While doing so I heard a message from the Beings of Light: "Although we all look different, we are all made of the same exact essence. We are Whole."

"Remember what the Indians taught us," I exclaimed to Gunter and Fernando. "*Hun Ol*," I chanted out loud and continued, "We are like the fingers and the hand. Each finger has a different function but they are all attached to the same hand. We are all together beating as one heart."

Then we looked at each other with one hand placed over our heart and said in Mayan, "*In Lak'esh* (I am you);" as the other replied, "*Ala K'in* (you are me)." Then we left the place feeling blessed.

Back in Colombia we gathered with the Maiz group, which by then numbered about forty people. We gave the rocks to the leader of the group, Herman Rodriguez, who put them all together into a beautiful ornate box, and then we showed them to everybody as we told the story.

One person raised their hand and proceeded to say with amusement, "I bet the red rock belongs to Gunter," as he pointed to Gunter's red hair, then everybody laughed.

"You are right," we answered.

"Can you guess the other two?" Gunter asked.

Everyone gave the correct answers. After the excitement I told everybody about the message of unity that I had received from the whole experience. They were very moved, and thanked us for sharing with them this amazing experience. That night during the meeting I felt closer to everyone else than I ever had before.

CHAPTER 22

Santiago and the Disappearance of the Body

I WAS meditating in my bed when I had a vision of a panoramic view of a bedroom where a man was resting on the bed. I didn't know where the room was, or the man's identity.

To which the Beings of Light answered, "You are going to meet."

"Why? Who is this guy? Where and when are we meeting?" I inquired.

"Soon, on campus. You are going to help each other a great deal."

As I came closer to him I was able to see his face clearly. His green eyes were bright and beautiful.

"Wow, he is a beautiful being. Okay, I want to meet him," I said, feeling joyful.

A couple of weeks later I met him at the cafeteria, where he was eating lunch with some of his buddies. When I saw him I recognized him immediately and I sat at the table right in front of him. I looked at him and as he returned a gaze into my eyes, I smiled. At first he barely smiled back, but after we looked at each other again we both smiled, then I stood up and waved goodbye.

We didn't talk that day, but later that week we met again at the cafeteria and then we introduced ourselves. His name was Santiago and he was studying Industrial Design.

His eyes were as profound and beautiful as in my vision, making me feel very comfortable in his presence. He liked me too, so we quickly became close friends. We dated for a couple of weeks until I told him that I really wasn't into the boyfriend-girlfriend kind of relationship; then we broke up. At the beginning, he didn't take the news well. But we had already learned so much about each other and felt so good together that we remained friends. For the very first time in Santiago's life, he had been able to talk openly with someone about his deepest feelings of sadness and anger, and I was so happy knowing that I was there, not just to listen, but offer guidance.

Santiago was born with a genetic defect that made his blood vessels grow abnormally on almost half of his body including his face. So, part of the left side of his face was covered with a dark purple blotch that he called "The Stain." Due to his condition he was very insecure about his appearance and was holding a lot of anger within himself. He couldn't understand why he had come into this harsh world to carry this kind of suffering. According to him, life was unfair.

When I met Santiago, he was a very analytical and skeptical person, which was something I was used to encountering. So when I first mentioned to him anything about metaphysics, he would always try to deny that anything in that realm was possible. This behavior soon stopped, when I told him that I was able to travel with my mind and see other places.

"Do you mean astral traveling? I have heard of that, but I don't believe it is possible," he exclaimed.

Then I proceeded to describe his bedroom in great detail to him, even though I had never been there in person. After his jaw dropped in disbelief, I told him something that I had once learned from the Beings of Light:

"Doubt everything, but always keep an open mind. An open mind has the potential to make great discoveries."

"Okay, I'll give it a try," he replied.

I told him about my spiritual groups, inviting him to come with me to TM and Maiz. After about two months into our friendship, he joined the groups and began to meditate for the very first time. Not long after, we started to experience amazing things together.

On one occasion when we were deeply immersed in a conversation about the chakras, I felt a tingling sensation in my hands. When I opened them right in front of Santiago, sparkles of light were coming from my palms. The light had the appearance of tiny sparks of light, shining very brightly, like glitter, before vanishing into the air. We looked at each other in amazement. After grabbing my hands he said, "I want some of that light."

"You already have it," I stated. "We are all surrounded by it. I told you already that I could see auras."

"I know for a fact that everything is made of matter and energy, but how is it possible that energy can manifest like that?"

"I am telling you, everything is possible. Just keep an open mind."

The same thing happened to us a few more times. Santiago would always try to find the most logical explanation, which sometimes led us into conflict.

"Ingrid, I am trying to have an open mind about all of this, but I think that these phenomena must have some kind of scientific explanation," he said.

"Stop putting rationality into everything," I would protest. "Not everything can be explained like that..."

"Yes, there is much about humanity that we still don't know," he interrupted, "but I am sure that everything has a logical explanation."

Still in disagreement, we decided not to discuss this issue anymore. *If he only knew half of the things I know he would realize how limited the rational mind can be,* I thought.

About a week later we met to go to a Maiz meeting together. On our way to catch the bus we had to walk a few blocks. We were distracted chatting when we saw three homeless people across the street, carrying big blankets around their bodies and looking disheveled.

When they noticed us, they crossed the street and came towards us. In Colombia, homeless people were responsible for much of the brutal street crimes. Feeling frightened, Santiago and I held each other's hands,

"Let's keep going, maybe they will let us go," Santiago whispered.

As they got closer I saw that they were all men. The closer they came, the more I invoked the presence of the Beings of Light.

When the three men surrounded us and started asking Santiago for his money, I realized that they were completely ignoring my presence, as if I wasn't even there. In fact, one of the men was right against my body while Santiago was being robbed. I was completely immobile, unable to talk or even blink. I didn't feel any emotions; I was only observing the scene.

The men asked Santiago for his watch, but he couldn't react. So they pulled his watch off his wrist, scratching his skin. Then they turned away and left. At that moment, I was able to move and talk. Feeling astonished I asked, "Santiago, are you okay? Your arm is bleeding."

He looked at me with his face still in shock and said, "I don't care about the watch or the money or my arm. None of that really matters. What really matters is what I have witnessed today. They didn't take anything from you because you were not here! This is something I cannot comprehend. This is completely out of my comprehension and my understanding."

"I don't know what happened either," I said. "Ever since I met you, incredible things have been occurring."

"All this is new to me. It is scary but also incredibly amazing. I think that I am going to stick with you!"

That day I couldn't wait to ask the Beings of Light about what had happened. Later that night they answered, "Sometimes extreme measures are required for the limited mind to get out of the way."

After knowing the Beings of Light for so many years I knew what they meant. "He is making himself ready for more. He is ready to expand, isn't he?"

"That's right. That is why you both met."

"Are extreme measures required for everyone?"

"Everyone is unique which makes every experience unique as well. Each person makes himself ready in his own way."

After this experience, Santiago and I became like a brother and sister. His mind certainly became more open and he started to explore, learn and use his own experiences, including his sufferings about his physical appearance — to teach and help others.

CHAPTER 23

Laughing as One

ONE DAY while talking with Santiago about the ego, I said, "I don't feel that I have an ego like everyone else."

"Just by you saying that you don't have an ego makes you have the biggest ego of all," he laughed.

I was quiet for a minute. "You know what, maybe you're right," and we both became silent. At that moment he looked at his watch and said, "It is time for me to go to class," and then left.

Sitting alone in the cafeteria I thought, *How silly of me! I must look pretty arrogant.* Of course I didn't mean to be arrogant; I just didn't know how to express that I felt detached from my persona most of the time, a feeling that I had known since my near-death experience. *How amazing it could be if Santiago could understand how it feels when one experiences unity? When all feelings of duality disappear, one becomes part of the Whole... I guess some day he will be ready.*

A few days later, Santiago met me at the house where we held Transcendental Meditation meetings every week. By this time, he had been practicing TM for six months. That night about thirty people were all gathered together in a big room. We sat on the floor with the lights off, in total silence.

Suddenly I did something that seemed opposed to everything I had learned about meditation: I started to giggle. No matter how hard I tried to stop, I just felt this unstoppable laugh emerging from within. Then one of my cousins who was sitting next to me started to laugh as well. We were followed by another and another, until the whole room was invaded by one loud, persistent and powerful roar of laughter. It became so contagious that even some people outside the room joined in. This was the longest and most intense laughter of my life, seeming to go on forever. According to someone waiting outside, it lasted for about twenty minutes.

Gradually we stopped laughing until the room became completely quiet, then stayed in meditation for another ten minutes. When the mediation ended, as we walked out of the room everybody wondered what had happened. People tried to find reasons but nobody could discover one. The common answer was that it had been the most amazing, liberating and unifying experience of our lives. That night, for no reason, we all simply laughed.

This was the first time that I had experienced such unity with so many people at the same time, without any effort or expectation whatsoever. After a minute of reflection, I realized: *This is what I meant to say the other day to Santiago. This is what I would call a moment without ego, without any sense of boundaries, or any separation or judgment; just a moment of unity, a moment of joy and love.*

Feeling grateful, I thanked the Beings of Light, then went to share my thoughts with my friend.

"Santiago, do you realize that it doesn't matter how different all of us are on the outside, because tonight we laughed as equals?"

"Wow! It was amazing. It felt like we were one big chorus," he said.

"Yes, we actually were!" I continued. "Do you also realize that this was a moment in which we were completely free from any judgment?"

"You're right. I could have never laughed like that if I thought I was being judged. This was definitely a gift."

"This is what I meant to say the other day at the cafeteria. That is what I would consider an egoless moment. Only by forgetting who we are and becoming free from judgment, can we let our True Self be."

"What is our True Self?" he asked.

At that moment, I remembered that the answer to that question had come to me about a year before, after I saw a movie on television about a person with amnesia. Feeling puzzled, I had asked the Beings of Light, "What would happen if I completely lost the memory of me, including my name? What would I become? Who would I be then? What would be left of me?"

"Your True Self," they answered.

I told Santiago about the movie and asked him the same questions. Looking baffled he answered, "I don't know."

"Think of yourself as an onion," I said. "An onion is made up of many layers, which is like the personality we have created after all these years of gathering experiences. The core of the onion is our beginning, a little baby who is pure and innocent. It is your True Self, totally naked and completely free from any conditions. But to get back to the heart of the onion, we need to first peel off all these outer layers. In total amnesia, you might go all the way to the beginning of the Self by accident. But what if you could consciously peel off all the layers? Instead of finding only an innocent and pure baby, you will find that you are also an all-knowing and wise baby."

"But, how do we do that?" he asked.

"You've already started," I answered. "Quieting your mind through meditation is the beginning. The quieter you become, the more aware you will be of your ego. That awareness will open the path for you to connect with your True Self and to learn the difference between *It* and the ego."

"So is the ego the enemy?"

"There is no enemy," I replied. Then I shared with Santiago more of what I had learned from the Beings of Light:

"The ego is but a tool that gives us the possibility to have an identity while we are in this world. This identity is not permanent because it can be changed and molded, while the True Self is our core essence, which remains permanent and unchanged. Just as the chameleon changes colors in order to blend with the environment, when I joined college I was able to change my personality in order to fit in. But no matter how many times the chameleon changes colors it remains the same chameleon. The important thing is to be aware and to always be clear that the ego is the tool and not the master. There is only one true master: *Self.*

"On the other hand, how could you know your True Self without the contrast of the ego? How could you know and appreciate health if you had never been sick? There is no enemy in the eyes of one who knows that everyone and everything has a loving purpose."

CHAPTER 24

Very Deep Into the Past

I WAS nineteen when my uncle invited me to a hypnosis event with a very experienced speaker. During the event, he asked for volunteers to be hypnotized, and from all the people who raised their hands, a few were randomly chosen. I didn't raise my hand, but my uncle pointed at me so vigorously that I ended up on the stage as well.

After I closed my eyes and he started to guide us through the experience, I drifted away to a state in which I felt completely peaceful, as if I was meditating. Then something unexpected happened: suddenly I could perceive the room from all different angles while sensing the energy emanating from everything that was present in a way similar to what happened when I was on Gorgona Island.

When the speaker realized that I wasn't following his guidance anymore he started the process to wake me up, but I wouldn't wake up. I was deeply enjoying the moment, and sensing the energy of an entire audience fixed on me.

"Wake up," I heard again, but I ignored his request. It felt great to realize that I wasn't terrified by the presence of all these people.

"Ingrid, wake up," he demanded one more time.

This time I paid attention to him; sensing his anxiety, I thought that it was time to come back. By then he was seriously stressed, and when I opened my eyes I sensed his relief. After all, we were standing in front of a big crowd and this wasn't part of the script.

"What happened? Where did you go?" he inquired.

"I don't know what happened, all I know is that I was feeling great. I am sorry, I didn't mean to scare you."

After that I thanked him and walked off the stage. At the end of the event some people asked me what happened, and all I said was that he had done a great job hypnotizing me.

My uncle later told me about a psychologist who used hypnosis. Since I was fascinated by what had happened and eager to learn more, he suggested that I should meet him.

The first time I went to meet the psychologist I told him about my experience during the hypnosis event. He suggested starting a session with a clear question about something I wanted to know or resolve, and from there he would guide me.

"I want to know why my health has always been so fragile," I said. Again things didn't go as expected. After a few seconds I began to experience profound peace, then suddenly visualized a child, whom I immediately recognized as the psychologist, sitting next to me.

"I see you," I said. "You are a child."

"What?" he exclaimed.

"Shush!" I whispered, "You are being bullied by people because of the look of your mouth. You feel sad and you have carried this trauma throughout your life. Even today you are afraid of laughing freely and loudly because you feel insecure, so you cover your mouth every time you laugh."

"How could you possibly know this?" he asked.

"Wait," I said. "I see that you have gone through many corrective procedures to fix your mouth, and even though your mouth looks perfectly normal now, you still carry this trauma. This affected you so much as a child that it has influenced almost every aspect of your life."

As I opened my eyes without his guidance I continued: "Doctor, it is time to move on, by letting go of the past and embracing your present you can be healed."

He was in complete awe because there was no way I could have known any of this information. I was pleasantly surprised as well. He suggested that I meet a friend of his, Dr. Guzman, who was a psychologist with expertise in hypnosis, and also a researcher of past life regressions.

Curious about what happened at the psychologist's office, that night I asked the Beings of Light what was going on.

"There is only one mind," was their first answer.

"But, why doesn't this happen with everyone else?"

"It does, but most people are not aware of it. In this case you two have consented to be aware of each other."

"What do you mean? This is the first time I saw this guy. I didn't know a thing about him."

"This is the first time you met physically, but you have already known each other in the non-physical realm" they answered.

"Like Santiago?" I asked.

"That's right. As you become ready you will meet everyone who you have consented to meet, even before you were born in this realm."

A couple weeks later when I met Dr. Guzman, he already knew from his friend what had happened. He also suggested that we should start with a clear question in mind. Since I had been experiencing some bad episodes of bronchitis, I wanted to know about my health once again. Why had I always experienced so many health problems, especially related to the respiratory system?

"How long have you been sick?" Dr. Guzman asked.

"Since I was a baby. My mom was extremely depressed during the whole pregnancy because my dad was gone, so she smoked tons of cigarettes and drank coffee…" After a pause I continued saying, "That's the reason why the doctors think I am sick, but I want to know if there is something else."

"Like what? What else is on your mind?"

I hesitated for a moment and said, "You are going to think that I am crazy, but I can remember with absolute clarity the first time I realized that I was breathing. I was just an infant."

"What happened?" he asked.

"I was lying on the bed and then I heard a loud sound, coming and going, but somehow a part of me. Now that I am older I could say that it was the first time of my life that I felt shock and fear. I wonder if that had anything to do with my health…"

Closing my eyes again and experiencing deep calm, I then started to feel extremely cold. I felt so frozen that my body was shaking, and I was having trouble trying to talk. Then suddenly I went back to the day when I was born, feeling very cold after being so warm in the womb. It was the same kind of cold I sensed when I fell into the deep tank as a child.

Then the intense coldness brought me to recognize myself in a prison cell in Italy, sentenced to die at the hands of the Inquisition. I was a man of faith and due to my spiritual beliefs, I had been brutally tortured and confined, alone and naked, in a dungeon room not much larger than my body, where I couldn't move. I sensed that I was in this hole for a long time until I finally died. I remember coughing intensely until the moment that I welcomed death.

That same day I was able to access two more past lives, and in all cases I had died from dreadful respiratory conditions. In those deaths the sound of my breathing had been loud, and I was in enormous pain and fear.

"This is the exact sound I heard, and the feelings I had when I became aware of my breathing as an infant," I said as I came to this realization.

After feeling very disturbed by the discovery, I suddenly experienced a deep sense of calmness and was ready to open my eyes.

"Wow, life has not been easy," I said to Dr. Guzman. "But somehow regardless of so much suffering and pain, I also feel a profound sense of release, like a big heavy weight has been removed from me."

At that moment I felt deeply grateful because I was finally able to understand the root cause of the intense coldness, the sickness, and the sadness that had been present throughout my current life. I was also able to perceive that there was an eternal, peaceful life prevailing beyond the sadness and sickness.

That day the cough that I had when I walked into Dr. Guzman's office simply disappeared, and I felt extremely healthy and energetic. Experiencing a healthy body was something incredible, new to me after nineteen years of feeling sick. I'd known since my NDE that my current life was just a continuation of a very long existence, but I didn't know I could have access to my other lives in a healing way.

"Remember, the body is a temporary shell, but life is eternal," the Beings of Light explained that night. "There is only one life; accessing those experiences is just a matter of remembering." Then they gave me a quick glimpse of some of my other past lives.

"Wow! This is totally amazing, but why do we forget in the first place?"

"Why wear the same old wardrobe when you have a completely

new and fresh one? You keep with you only what is essential for growing, and you let go of the rest. Think of how hard it would be for the mind to allow new experiences and to evolve if it was completely focused on the past."

"That makes sense. But how could I start this day feeling so sick, and after accessing these memories, suddenly feel renewed and healed?" I wondered.

"Darkness cannot prevail in the light of awareness. Once you have a clear view of an obstacle, your path through it is obvious," they stated.

"That fast?"

"It could take longer, but why delay?"

"This is absolutely fascinating," I said feeling astounded.

"Keep visiting Dr. Guzman. You both have much to learn from each other," the Beings of Light suggested.

During a few more visits to Dr. Guzman, I was able to access many other life experiences, wherein I was able to perceive other sad events, but also some very happy moments as well. We helped each other a great deal as he advanced in his research about past-life regressions, and I became aware that it was possible to access deeper levels of the unconscious mind to heal the mind and body. From the very first visit to Dr. Guzman, the chronic bronchitis that I'd experienced since infancy was gone, and never returned.

CHAPTER 25

The Power of Trust and Willingness

ON A long holiday weekend during my second year of college, some friends and I planned to visit a lake located high in the Colombian Andes, called Iguaque Flora and Fauna Sanctuary. Iguaque was a sacred place to the indigenous people known as Muisca. According to their legends this lake was the place where mankind originated. This park has been considered among the calmest places on earth.

We were supposed to be a group of six, but since this was a last-minute plan, the girlfriends of two of my friends couldn't come. So I ended up being the only girl in the group. Kevin, Mauricio, Oscar and I left on a Thursday evening with all we needed for a three-day camping trip.

While riding on the bus, I learned from Kevin that we were not going to reach the lake by following the traditional hiking path from the entrance of the park, but would instead start from a near-by village. He said that he knew the path so we didn't argue. The village was located about 8,800 feet above sea level, and the lagoon at 12,500, so we knew that we had a long way to go.

We arrived at the small village about 6:00 a.m., and after talking to some locals we were reassured that it would only take about half a day to get to the lake. We started our way up trying to avoid areas of dense forest, so we could keep the top of the mountain in view. The path was very steep and once we arrived there, we realized that there was much farther to go. We could see many mountains peaking on the horizon, and there was not a clear path to follow. Kevin seemed very confident, so we kept walking along with him.

As we kept climbing higher, the land became more arid and the vegetation started to change going from tall, moss-covered trees and ferns to shorter trees and small shrubs. We knew that we had reached the level of the Paramo, a type of Andean ecosystem that's found at 11,000 feet. The air also became depleted of oxygen, making everybody feel heavier and more tired by the minute. It was about noon when we stopped to eat lunch and after a short rest we kept walking. Kevin kept assuring us that by now we had to be very close to our goal, but the hours kept passing and there wasn't a lake to be seen.

About two in the afternoon, after walking for eight hours, we finally said to Kevin that maybe we were lost and he admitted that we might be. We had to decide whether to continue or go back, then decided to walk for a little longer in case we were close. We kept saying, "Maybe the lake is on the other side of that mountain," but as we advanced we saw only more mountains. The temperature was dropping drastically and we were getting very tired, so we decided to go back. A couple hours later, we realized that we were completely lost.

As the sun started to set and the temperature kept going down, we could feel the wind penetrating into our bones like needles. The terrain was very rocky and steep so we decided that it was probably safer to stop for the day. We looked for a spot in a valley where the wind was less intense so we could set up the tent and make a fire. The night was so cold that we decided that it was better to join the sleeping bags and snuggle all together. That way nobody would freeze during the night. That night we didn't talk much, and went to sleep feeling worried and tense.

Early Saturday morning we had breakfast, packed everything and continued walking. It wasn't until noon, when we were going to eat lunch, that Mauricio suggested, "We should ration the food because we don't know how long we are going to remain in these mountains." After agreeing, we ate small portions and walked the entire day until the night arrived. By then, we were all exhausted, hungry, and very frightened.

Two days had passed and time was beginning to stretch out. Oscar was worried: "What if we never make it back? I have heard of many people who got lost in the Andes. What if we become part of the statistics?" One of the ideas that scared us the most was that nobody knew where we were. Since we didn't use the main entrance of the park, no one had seen us embark on our journey. So our disappearance would probably be an unsolved mystery. At this point, it was up to us to discover the way back without help.

That night, I prayed to God and the Beings of Light to help us find our way back. In the middle of the night I woke up with the memory of my cousin and I starting a fire in a small bedroom while playing camp.

"The power of a mind free of fear enabled you to extinguish that fire. Trust yourself and you will be able to provide the guidance needed to find the way back," the Beings of Light said.

"They are three strong and smart guys," I protested. "Why would they look for my guidance? I am just a girl!" I was still conditioned to the cultural mindset that men were leaders and women followers. I felt this way especially with this group of college friends, who were not at all into spirituality. That night I recognized how challenging it was still for me to feel oneness with the non-believers. But once again the Beings of Light gave me the awareness that I needed.

"You are also a strong and smart girl. The only difference between you and them is in your mind," they affirmed.

"Okay, I will try," I agreed.

I woke up Sunday morning feeling extremely energetic and ready to continue. I said to the guys, "I know that we are going to make it. The important thing is not to give up." For the rest of that day, and Monday, I never felt scared, tired, thirsty, or hungry. I felt that nothing could affect me no matter what difficulties we were facing, especially because at this point of my life I felt healthier than ever. I remember being able to walk for hours without feeling the need to stop, and a few times I caught myself leading the guys.

The fourth day, late on Monday, while walking through a very steep area, Mauricio lost his balance and fell a few feet down a hill, hurting his right ankle. Then we had to slow down. He had to support himself with a stick to be able to walk, but his ankle was swelling and he started to feel intense pain. So, that day we were forced to stop early. As we had done the previous nights we descended into a valley to set up the tent. The sun was already going down, and when we went to turn on the flashlight it wasn't working anymore, so that evening we had to work mostly in the dark.

That particular night the wind was pretty strong, producing very loud noises. In the middle of this ordeal, Kevin said, "If we were to die here, at least it would happen in the company of good friends and in a place that resembles paradise."

"Don't think that way, we are not going to die here," I affirmed.

Regardless, we all agreed that we had seen some of the most amazing things nature could offer. Mighty skies adorned with infinite amounts of stars at night, astonishing sunsets and sunrises, incredible landscapes of endless mountain peaks and valleys, all under the most profound peace, quiet, and serenity one could hope to experience.

Despite the new obstacles, I didn't focus on the circumstances and instead kept my mind centered on the Beings of Light's message: *Everything is going to be fine. Remember that you are not alone.*

When we woke up Tuesday morning Kevin had a new idea, "Since Mauricio is hurt I think that the best thing to do is to split up. Somebody will stay with Mauricio while the other two will go and look for help," he suggested. After we flipped a coin, I was the one who had to stay. Then Kevin pointed toward the rising sun and said, "That is the way we are going."

"That is not the way we were going yesterday," Oscar challenged.

"I am following my gut," Kevin replied.

"I trust him," I said.

We could have chosen not to believe him because he was the one who got us lost in the first place, but that day I trusted his feelings. At this point there was nothing to lose and following somebody's gut was better than nothing. If he was talking from the heart, we needed to listen.

As Kevin and Oscar were climbing a very steep mountain, I was sitting at the entrance of the tent feeling confident that they were going to come back and bring help. I never doubted the Beings of Light; however, I was still anxious because I didn't know how long we would be there waiting. Our food supply was running out, as we were supposed to be gone for three days and it was now five. Looking very worried Mauricio said to me, "I feel so guilty that you had to stay behind because of me."

"You do not need to worry everything is all right. We are not alone. God is going to bring us back home," I answered, feeling confident.

"I hope so… thank you!" he sighed.

Mauricio went back into the tent to rest while I stayed at the tent entrance looking at Kevin and Oscar becoming tiny as they hiked toward the mountain peak. This was the first time in days that I was able to sit and have a long rest. It wasn't until then that I realized that the ends of my socks were all bloody. When I pulled them off I found that most of my toenails were bruised and a few had fallen off, but I never had felt any pain. So I decided not to think about it and put my socks back on. I closed my eyes and meditated, praying for strength.

Suddenly I heard the sound of shouting voices far in the distance, and when I looked up I saw the guys at the very top of the mountain waving their arms. I knew at that moment that they had found our way out. Then I called for Mauricio, and stood up jumping and waving back at them while thanking God and the Beings of Light. As they started to come back down the hill, I said to Mauricio, "See, you don't need to feel bad because thanks to your accident we were forced to stay in this valley, and to trust Kevin's gut."

"Thanks Ingrid, for being so kind."

"I have learned in my life that everything happens for a good reason."

"That is a good way to experience life," Mauricio replied.

Kevin and Oscar had made the decision to come and get us instead of trying to spend who knows how long trying to find help. They came back laughing and yelling, "After all this, we found the lake!"

Due to Mauricio's injury it took a while to get to the lake, but despite the pain he barely complained. The fact that we were getting out of this predicament was more important than anything else. At the lake we found two park rangers who helped us go all the way to the entrance of the park, and from there we made it back to the city. Once in the city some of us had to deal with some worried and angry parents and girlfriends, but in the end the only thing that mattered was that we were back alive.

Days later while talking to Mauricio he said to me, "I have a confession to make... the only reason why we didn't complain much, or express much fear while we were lost, was because of you."

"What did I do?" I asked feeling surprised.

"Although you were the smallest and skinniest of the group and appeared to be the most fragile you never complained. Your attitude remained so positive, giving us the strength we needed to keep going."

"Thanks for telling me this," I replied. "You can't imagine how much I appreciate it. Overtime I have learned that the way we use our minds can bring us to our success or our demise. It is entirely our choice, no matter how strong or fragile we appear to be on the outside. Thanks to this experience, now I know that the disadvantages of being a girl are only beliefs stuck in my mind."

I felt grateful to the Beings of Light for showing me one more time that it was possible to bypass the limitations of the mind, as well as the sufferings of the body. We can work with the power of the unlimited mind to achieve the unthinkable.

CHAPTER 26

The Paradox of Time and Reality

URING my second year of college, my involvement with all my spiritual groups ended. Agni Yoga dissolved because of low membership, and I stopped going to the TM meetings because I learned that the married leader of the group tried to seduce my oldest sister, Lis. My sister and I felt very sad and disappointed, and decided to walk away. Soon after, his TM group broke up when it was discovered that he was benefiting from charging large sums of money to the members, which made me feel even more sorrowful because I had deeply trusted this man. But I did what the Beings of Light had taught me: *Don't judge... and keep walking.*

The last group I stopped visiting was Maiz. One night during a family reunion, after having too much to drink, my dad confessed to me: "I am dating someone in Maiz and I think that I am in love."

"What? Who is this person?" I asked, feeling very disturbed.

After divulging her name, he made me promise that I wouldn't tell my mom. At that moment I understood why his attitude at home had been so aggressive and negative for the past few months. I felt so sad for my mom that I couldn't go back to Maiz, knowing what I had learned.

During those days I had made a new friend named Angelica,

and she and her family became my refuge. To cheer me up they often took me out to dance and party, which seemed to work since I loved dancing. I was still living with my parents, but between the time I spent in college and with Angelica I was barely seen at home anymore.

"This house is not a hotel!" my mom yelled at me once.

"Mom, college is too hard," I answered. "I'm busy studying but I will try to be here more often." I hugged her and gave her a kiss. I knew she missed me but I just couldn't be at home and see my mom suffering while I was holding this terrible secret.

Life at home was absolute chaos. Besides what was happening with my parents, my two younger sisters were totally misbehaving, getting involved with the wrong crowds. It seemed that nothing was going right. I felt so angry at my dad because I felt that all of this was his fault. At this point in my life I really wondered how could I live a spiritual life together in the midst of all this conflict.

One evening while riding the bus back home from college I was thinking, *This is all like a bad dream from which I'd like to wake up. I wish that all of this was not real!* I felt strongly that I was just a passenger observing the world, the same way I was sitting on the bus observing the road. Then all of a sudden everything around me, including my own body, started to turn into trillions of very tiny moving particles, like sparks of vibrant energy.

First, I realized that the bus wasn't just a solid, well-defined, massive object. It was made up of individual particles, both organic and inorganic, moving in space. The particles had various colors and vibrations, and even produced different sounds that maintained them grouped together, giving every object its own distinctive signature. As the vibrations of all the particles started to change, their forms began to lose shape until everything, including my body, fused into one big bright cloud of particles. Even the noise produced by all the different shapes turned into a unique sound when everything was fused together. In the end, all that remained was empty bright space. For a brief moment before everything returned to its original shape, there was nothing. I have found that it is impossible to explain what nothing means, but it basically signifies the absence of sound, form, color, feeling, or meaning. The strange thing was that although my body had vanished somehow, I was still there, *Being*.

After returning from this astonishing experience I thought, *Wow, it is one thing to sense oneness with other beings, but another to feel it with other objects!* I was simply perplexed: *Why and exactly when did we stop knowing that we are one with the Whole? How is it even possible to forget what we really are?*

After this moment of wonder and clarity, other thoughts and complaints filled my mind: *If nothing is real why are we even here? Why is this human experience so hard? Why is it really needed? Why is this happening to me?*

"In twenty years you will understand," the Beings of Light answered.

"Twenty years, you have to be kidding me! That is an eternity," I said, feeling disappointed.

After that, nothing more happened that day. The communication simply stopped and I arrived at my destination. At nineteen years old I couldn't conceive of waiting twenty years to get answers. It seemed like forever and a day. *It has to be a mistake*, I thought. But a couple of days later the Beings of Light gave me the message again, very clearly.

I was walking out of the cafeteria's bathroom at college when I bumped into my Ethics professor, whom I truly admired. After we apologized, we kept walking side-by-side making our way out of the cafeteria. As we were walking I mentioned to him how much I liked his class, and how interesting I found all the concepts that he had taught us. He was a very serious and focused kind of person, and after listening to my words he stopped walking and turned to me saying, "Twenty years will pass before you understand the real meaning of these teachings." I stood there looking at him in complete silence.

Then he continued, "Now you are standing on my left, but in twenty years you will be on the right."

"What do you mean?" I asked, feeling disconcerted.

"Give it about twenty years," he insisted. "The day you change the way you perceive things, you will have more answers than questions."

"Why twenty years?" I said exasperated.

"Every ten years we complete a cycle of change and maturity. For what I know about you, you will need at least two more cycles."

Subsequently, he excused himself saying that he was in a hurry and perhaps we could resume the conversation later. So he walked away and left me standing in the middle of a big open hall with more questions and no answers.

Still after a moment of quietness, his words helped me to remember a profound Zen teaching. It was a story of a monk named Tenno, who after ten years of apprenticeship achieved the rank of Zen Master. One rainy day, he went to visit a famous master named Nan-in. Once inside the master asked him a question, "Did you leave your wooden clogs and umbrella on the porch?" After he answered yes, Nan-in continued asking, "Did you place your umbrella to the left of your shoes, or to the right?" He couldn't give him an answer because he couldn't remember. Tenno realized that he had not yet attained full awareness, and became Nan-in's apprentice for another ten years.

"Is this what you are trying to tell me, that to attain full awareness I need more time?" I asked the Beings of Light. But there was no answer.

On my way to catch the bus I heard them saying, "Some day you will pass these teachings onto many others."

"I don't think I could ever be a teacher."

"You already are, but to get where you want to go, you are giving yourself time."

"What do you mean that I am giving myself time? You are the ones who said twenty years."

"We are only making you aware of your deep desires. You are the one designing and creating your own reality. As you saw on the bus, nothing is as it appears to be."

The Beings of Light were absolutely right. All I wanted at the time was to be normal like everyone else. The end of my involvement with all the spiritual groups and the problems at home had led me to meet new people and enter a world of new experiences that I was enjoying. Besides, recently I had also met the first guy in my life to turn my world upside down. He didn't know anything about my spirituality and I wanted to keep it that way. So, who was I trying to fool? I also recognized that I had been feeling guilty because I had been pushing aside the Beings of Light.

"Sometimes the only way to find peace and reconciliation is to walk away from everything you know, and experience new things," they said. "You are not doing anything to us, this is all for you."

"Thanks for understanding me and for giving me clarity," I replied, feeling relieved.

"Soon you will not see us for a while."

"I feel conflicted because although I want to be by myself I don't want you to go."

"You know we are here."

"I know… thanks for letting me go."

From that day on, I gradually stopped hearing and seeing the Beings of Light and got very busy studying, partying, meeting new people, and falling in love.

CHAPTER 27

Falling in Love and Leaving Home

TOWARDS the end of my second year of college Angelica and Santiago had become the closest people to me, until I met Jaime. He seemed to embody the complete opposite of my ideal for someone I would date. I thought that the man of my life was going to be someone very spiritual, in tune with nature, a giver, a peacekeeper, a lover… but instead I walked into the path of one of the most popular guys in college, who was a part of a Death Metal band and seemed interested only in partying and having fun. However, from the moment I met him I totally surprised myself, because I became crazy about this man.

I met Jaime not long before the Beings of Light had told me that I needed twenty years to understand the teachings. By then I didn't feel strongly attached to anything. I didn't care about possessions, or trends, or sports. I didn't feel the need to sleep much. I barely felt hungry or thirsty. In fact, I wasn't attracted to any kind of food or beverage. To me eating was only a matter of keeping my body functioning. At this point my sexuality was also dormant. In the years when everyone's hormones were at their highest peaks, I was not concerned about dating anyone or having sex. My biggest thirst revolved around understanding humanity and myself. Even during the time when my involvement with all the spiritual groups ended, I was still very involved in spirituality, but thinking that my spiritual and secular worlds were in conflict.

Nobody introduced us. I just saw him standing in a corridor at college, and from that very moment I fell hard for him. He had big brown and very expressive eyes, long black hair, and a very athletic body. But the most important thing was that he had a bright and beautiful aura. I couldn't stop thinking about him, but when I learned who he was I reasoned: *Why would he be interested in someone like me?* I always perceived myself as physically unattractive, since I grew up hearing how beautiful my sisters were. During my teenage years the feeling of not being attractive was reinforced when I realized that boys were very attracted to my sisters. No matter how many times I have learned that external appearance was not important, that was not what the world of romance was showing me. To me it looked like a very competitive market, owned by the prettiest. So the idea of being so different from him, besides not feeling pretty, strongly resurfaced.

Not long after I saw him for the first time, I was able to overcome my fears and talk to him. We met at the college library when we both got in line to borrow books, and after gathering enough courage I started a conversation. Once we talked I was happy to discover that he was an amusing and nice guy, as reflected by his aura. From that day on we started to bump into each other more often and became friends. One day I went to his house to visit and we ended up making love for the first time. That day I felt the deepest sense of love and connection I had ever felt for anyone in my life, but since we didn't know each other that well I didn't say a word.

We became what was known as "friends with benefits," because Jaime was not interested in dating. I was okay with it. The fact that he liked me and wanted to hang out was good enough. Still, he meant a great deal to me. I stopped going to any spiritual gatherings that interfered with his parties and concerts. I was listening to music I never cared about before, and going to bars and clubs I never intended to visit. I started to live in a world that was completely unknown to me, and surprisingly I was enjoying it because he was a part of it. I became so infatuated that I wanted to be with him all the time, yet he didn't feel the same for me. I would wait for him at the end of the day after completing all the classes, and tried to go to his band practices as often as I could.

After about two months of hanging out together, one day we met on a staircase at college and he said, "You are getting too close to me. I am starting to feel suffocated. I almost feel that you are stalking me."

"I'm sorry, I never intended to make you feel this way," I said, as my heart was feeling punctured.

"Don't take it wrong. I just need space."

"It's okay, I get it." In fact I'd never felt this much pain in my life before. Despite wanting to be with him so badly, I decided not to talk to him again. I felt so stupid for allowing myself to get too close to someone who didn't really want to be with me. Seeing him in the distance was a torture, so before it got worse I pleaded during my prayers not to see him again. Just like that, we stopped crossing each other's paths, despite being at the same small campus. Although I hadn't seen or talked to the Beings of Light for a while I always thought about them, so I thanked them for answering my plea to keep Jaime out of my sight.

Those days I discovered that although my self-esteem about my looks was low, my sense of pride was otherwise very high. I kept living my life trying to enjoy and deeply appreciate Angelica's friendship, which helped me to overcome my ongoing family troubles, my broken heart, and the fact that I terribly missed the Beings of Light. Sometimes I wondered if walking away from them had been a terrible mistake, although they told me that this was the best for me.

About eight months after not exchanging a word with Jaime, I met him by accident at a restaurant. The place was crowded and when a table became available, we both ran for it at the same time. When I realized that it was him we looked at each other with amazement. It felt like a million butterflies were fluttering in my stomach.

"Would it be okay if we share the table?" he asked.

A myriad of thoughts crossed my mind within a second, and with them the realization that I was still having very strong feelings for him. He looked at me with an apologetic expression in his eyes and waited until I answered: "It's okay, I guess we can share the table."

"I feel so sorry for the way I treated you, and the hurtful words I said to you the last time we talked," he said.

"It's okay, I got it. You didn't want to be with me in the same way I wanted to be with you. I never intended to suffocate you. It was best just to walk away."

"I saw you a few times during the past months, but I felt too ashamed to talk to you. I want you to know that I have missed you."

"Missed me, why?"

"You are the most amazing girl I have ever met. You accepted me the way I am. You never criticized me or patronized me or tried to change me in any way. You let me be. You are also the most optimistic, happiest, loving and caring person I know. I feel free and happy when I am with you."

Even though that day I felt as happy as a puppy, I was afraid to get hurt again. Consequently, although I told him that he could call me, I kept rejecting all his invitations until one day he invited me out again and said, "If you don't come this time, it will be clear to me that you don't want us to hang out. I will understand if you don't."

That day I decided that I wanted to give it one more chance, and I am glad I did because after that we had the best time we could have ever asked for. We became more open and honest with each other, and enjoyed together every bit of life.

Not long after our reunion he told me something I had never heard from another person in this life: "I love you."

Listening to these words, especially coming from him, caused me to start crying.

"I love you too," I told him as we hugged.

In Colombia couples often use the term "I like you," so if someone says, "I love you," they really meant it.

"Why are you crying?" he asked.

"I know that my family and friends love me but I have never heard these words said to me before. My parents didn't grow up hearing them so they never said them to me."

I was overwhelmed with emotion because finally I was able to express my feelings freely, and to sense that my love for him was being reciprocated.

The longer we hung out the more I realized that the reason I felt so attracted to Jaime from the very beginning was his uniqueness. He didn't care at all about being normal; in fact he didn't want to be normal. At the time in Colombia a man with long hair and earrings wasn't socially accepted, even less if he listened to heavy metal since this kind of music was considered satanic. In him I saw what I was afraid to be.

After we grew closer I told him some things about my spirituality, although we didn't talk about it too much, because we were mostly hanging out with friends and having fun. Being with him helped me to realize that I was still carrying my spirituality with me wherever I was. Even though I wasn't part of any group or reading spiritual books anymore, I had continued living my life with the same spiritual principles that had directed me for the past twenty years. By being with Jaime, I started to recognize that being myself was what really mattered.

* * *

Becoming a marine biologist required moving next to the sea for two additional years. After spending three years of college living in Bogota with my parents, it was time to move to the Caribbean Coast of Colombia to a city called Santa Marta. Leaving Jaime was a complete torture; we had been dating for about a year and having a blast. The last few weeks before my departure, we spent every minute we could together, sharing emotions from happiness to complete desolation.

"I know you have to go because your career is your life," he said, crying, the day before I left. I had never seen a man cry in front of me before.

"You are my life too," I replied, feeling devastated. "We are going to make it. I know we can do it."

"I hope so," he sobbed as he gave me a gift. It was a diving knife. "This is for your safety, and to think about me when you are diving." That day we wept inconsolably. Leaving Jaime was not the only challenge I faced. During those days, my parent's marriage finally ended, after twenty-four years of struggle. Two weeks before I left home, my dad took me and two of my sisters on a short weekend vacation, where unbeknownst to us, he had planned to meet his lover. Someone who knew about my dad's plan told my mom while we were gone. At home with my younger sister, she felt so angry and devastated that she collected everything she could from the house and left before we returned. I was destroyed. I wished I would have told her the truth about my dad's affair long before, but I just couldn't. Not just because I had made a promise to my dad, but also because I knew that she was still in love with him. I couldn't be the source of this horrible news.

Besides, I kept hoping that this was just a short phase in my dad's life. This wasn't the first time my dad had an affair. When I was six years old, he took my sisters and me to a pizza place, where a blonde woman was waiting for us. "I am going to introduce you to someone important to me," he said pointing to her at a table.

"Who is she, daddy?" we asked.

"Your future mother."

I couldn't comprehend what was happening. I felt so distraught that I didn't want to talk or eat any pizza. Back at home I prayed so hard to God for her to go away because I didn't want to have another mother. Thankfully, after a while she did leave my dad, and my parents got back together.

At twenty-one, I couldn't pray anymore for them to stay together. I had seen so much suffering at home that for me it seemed best if they parted. After my mom left we didn't know where she had gone or how she was doing. We talked to her parents but they didn't reveal anything to us. We missed our mom terribly but my sisters and I couldn't cry when my dad was around, because according to him, crying was a sign of weakness.

"Don't cry, be strong, nothing is happening," he always said.

So I left home without seeing my mom, not being able to

express my feelings freely. I wanted to see her and ask for forgiveness because I felt I had betrayed her. During those days every bit of my heart was broken.

The financial situation at home, which had been at chaos for a long while, only worsened with my parents' separation. Thankfully, I had a government loan that paid for college, and I had worked little jobs here and there, so I had a little cash saved for the expenses of moving to my new home.

As if all this wasn't enough, this was a time when the political situation in Colombia was very unstable. While the Government was trying to negotiate peace agreements with two of the most important revolutionary groups, the rebels continued attacking small villages, blowing up bridges, massacring and kidnapping people left and right. During those days, traveling by bus or car between cities presented a great deal of risk. Yet, due to the financial situation at home, I didn't have any other option than bus travel.

Since I had already said my goodbyes to my best friends, Santiago and Angelica, my boyfriend Jaime, and my sisters, my dad was the only one taking me to the bus station. None of my friends came with me to the Caribbean because they were all studying Industrial Design. Before boarding the bus I said to my dad, "I wished for a while that you and mom could get back together as you had before."

"I only stayed with her because of you. I wouldn't leave my daughters as my mom left me... sorry, but I wasn't in love with your mom," he confessed.

When I boarded the bus he patted me on the shoulder and we said goodbye. My dad didn't grow up surrounded by much affection, so at the time he was not very affectionate. That day I experienced the worse feelings of sadness and sorrow in my life.

The bus trip to Santa Marta was going to take at least twenty-three hours. Along the way we encountered several police and military checkpoints where all vehicles had to stop for security checks. There was a lot of anxiety among the people on the bus, because at first glimpse it was not possible to discern if the checkpoints were held by government forces or rebel forces. After about sixteen hours of travel, it was very late at night when almost everyone had fallen asleep due to exhaustion. Then the kind of situation we feared the most was in front of us. As the bus reached the top of a mountain, the driver spotted a fire far in the distance. Since he had some experience with this kind of situation, he decided to turn the lights off and stop the bus behind a semi-truck that was parked on the side of the road. The driver of the truck said that the rebels had burned several buses; they were fighting the military just ahead of us. So he suggested that we all wait. There was nothing else our driver could do; the road comprised only two narrow lanes, with a steep mountain on one side and a cliff on the other. There was no turning back.

In the distance we could hear intense gunfire. "I suggest that you crouch and stay in your seats until the situation is clear," the bus driver shouted. The bus was filled with an atmosphere of extreme fear. Crouched in my seat for almost nine hours in total discomfort, I cried like never before, praying to the Beings of Light for the well-being of my family back at home, and myself. Thankfully, the victory was for the military forces, but not without the cost of lives on both sides, and some innocent bystanders.

What a way to start my life away from home. Could things get even worse? I thought. For a while, they did. I didn't have a penny in my pocket and being away from home with no money proved to be a very hard challenge. To make matters worse, the university didn't have dorms and living in the city was quite expensive. To reduce expenses, three classmates and I rented an apartment. They wanted to live in a very nice condominium located close to the university. It was at the top of my budget but I had to take it because at the time I didn't feel that I had any other option. Classes were about to start, and everyone else had already settled with their own roommates.

From the beginning of the semester I really struggled with money. Sometimes I didn't have enough to get toiletries, only the basics of food and rent. However, I was grateful to God and the Beings of Light because throughout my life I had learned to live with little. Regardless of my hardship I was living in a very beautiful resort area. I didn't bother looking for a job because the college program was too intense. So, I tried to feel the best I could with the little I had.

Back then, the only thing that could really bring me down was missing my loved ones back home. But when I would recall the ongoing family dramas, I'd realize I was better off where I was. It was clear to me that things were not going to be easy, but to remain positive I focused on being aware and appreciative of all the little things that made my life better. In all those things I could perceive the loving, everlasting presence of the Beings of Light, without whom I would have felt utterly lost.

CHAPTER 28

Angels Along the Path

L EAVING home was probably the best thing that could have happened for me at the time, since family conflicts kept becoming more complex. After a couple of weeks away, I finally got a call from my mom. It was a short call because she was financially broken. Hearing her voice and talking to her felt good, but I knew that everyone at home was living their own version of hell. Despite the family chaos and my own struggles, I kept myself together against almost insurmountable odds.

A few weeks into the semester, one afternoon while feeling down I decided to join a group of classmates for a walk on the beach. While walking we saw in the distance a very handsome man coming towards us. All of us started to whisper and giggle. When he passed by us, he pointed at me, saying with a smile, "I have seen you before."

"Who, me?" I questioned.

"Yes you, I saw you a few days ago at the ice cream shop."

I didn't remember seeing such a handsome man anywhere before, nor had the girls mentioned anything about seeing any attractive guy at the shop.

"I don't remember seeing you," I replied blankly.

"You were the only one not eating ice cream," he said.

Then one of the girls touched my back and whispered, "Just

talk to him…. We will be over there waiting for you."

They left us alone. After talking with him for only a few minutes, he managed to lift my mood. I felt something familiar and comfortable about him, so we stayed on the beach conversing for a while. He was a very charming guy with intense bright eyes; his aura was very bright, wide and beautiful.

"Why weren't you eating ice cream? Don't you like it?" he teased.

"Sometimes I do, but I don't like sugar much." Then after a pause I said, "So you really saw me at the ice cream shop!"

"Of course, I did. Did you think that I was lying?"

"Maybe!"

And then we both laughed. It had been a while since I laughed, and enjoyed someone's company this much.

After talking for a little while longer he asked, "Why don't you have a bicycle like the rest of your friends?"

"Okay, I'll tell you the truth. It's the same reason that I didn't eat ice cream a few days ago, because I can't afford it… that is the truth."

Usually I wouldn't have been that open to strangers, but he made me feel like it was okay to share. When it was time to go, I told him about the place where I was living and that he was welcome to visit us anytime. He radiated such a good and intense energy that his presence lasted several days for me.

The very next day I left early to go to class, and when I came back in the evening I was approached by the condominium's guard, who told me that somebody had left me a present. Then he asked me to wait. I couldn't believe my eyes when he showed up with a brand new beautiful red bicycle. It had a message attached to it saying:

"When you don't need it anymore leave it behind. It was great talking to you at the beach. Enjoy it!"

I felt very grateful and excited at first, but then I started to question myself about whether this guy wanted something in return for this present. At the time, I was still very much in love with Jaime, so going out with someone else was out of the question. However, as the days passed I actually started to wonder if I would ever see the beach boy once more. Weeks passed, and I never saw him again.

Eventually I began to question if this meeting had been the work of the Beings of Light! I felt so grateful and joyous riding that bike. This gift was enough to bring up my spirits for the rest of the semester. Once more the Beings of Light had shown me that I was never alone, and they were taking care of me.

* * *

Near the end of my first semester living in Santa Marta, Jaime came from Bogota to visit me. During his vacation, he wanted to explore some of the stunning beaches close to a small fishing village called Taganga. So, one Saturday morning we packed our snorkeling gear and headed for the beach. To get there, we first had to ascend and then descend a steep mountain path. The view of the beaches from the top was breathtaking. As far as the eyes could see, there were countless small, white-sand beaches enclosed by cliffs. They looked like little sanctuaries.

Once we reached the ocean, we snorkeled for a while and after resting on the sand, we decided to go for a walk to explore some of the other beaches. To cross from one beach to the other we had to climb a few rocks, most of which were covered with pink algae that made them very slippery. Sometimes it was necessary to wade through the surf. We probably had visited five or six beaches when we reached a very small one, enclosed by a sharp cliff making it hard to go farther. At this point we decided to go back, but before leaving we sat on the sand and chatted for a little while about this beautiful paradise.

As we started to head back, crossing around the rocky edge of a cliff, we met face-to-face with three men. As soon as I saw them, I sensed that they intended to harm us. One of the men slid on a slippery rock and almost fell down; Jaime grasped his arm and said, "Be careful." I thought that this act of kindness might persuade the man from hurting us, but that was not the case. They pushed us backwards toward the water, while two of them got some large knives and a piece of broken glass out of their pockets. They demanded all our belongings. After taking everything from us, they tied Jaime's hands behind his back with some rope and forced him to sit on the beach. As one man was tying Jaime's hands, another was holding the piece of glass to his neck.

Jaime started to yell at the men, "Leave her alone, you don't need to hurt her. You already have our things; isn't that enough?" Meanwhile I was standing on the beach petrified, completely quiet and still, observing all that was happening. Then I turned my head toward the ocean to stop seeing the brutality of the scene, and as my tear-filled eyes saw the calm waters of the ocean, I shifted from a state of total fear to contemplation. I saw the most beautiful deep blue horizon that I had ever seen, then thought: *This is a good day to die.* I already knew that I wasn't scared of dying, but I didn't know how ready I was. Ever since my near-death experience I had been ready for the day I would have to go.

At that moment, I felt the same calm and tranquility that I had felt a few years prior, when I was ambushed by two men on the street. As Jaime kept yelling at the men, they also tied my hands behind my back and violently pushed me to the ground. I felt completely numb and emotionless. My head became empty of thought and I never sensed for even a second that I would be raped or further harmed. The leader of the group was a strong, tall, muscular man, with dark skin and very distinctive tattoos on his chest and arm. I was hyper-aware of every detail; even today I can precisely recall every aspect of this man from the shape of his eyes to the color of his skin and the smell of his body.

He placed his body on top of mine and moved his hand towards my groin. I knew that this guy had to be very heavy because he looked twice Jaime's size, but I could not feel the weight of his body. As he started to touch me, somehow I freed my right hand as if it had not been tied up at all. Gently but powerfully, I grabbed his lower jaw, positioning his face so his eyes met directly with mine. I saw a very bright light emerging from all around us, then I felt the voice of the Beings of Light talking through me. In a very soft, calm, but firm manner, the voice said to him, "Dear, you do not want to do this to me."

The man jolted, moving his body away from me while my eyes were still piercing his. He looked confused and disoriented, then yelled at the other guys, "Let's go, we are out of here!" The other two didn't dare challenge him, and they all fled. It was absolutely amazing how these peaceful words were able to end such aggressive and evil intentions.

I stood up quickly with the clear knowledge that the ordeal had not yet ended. I untied Jaime's hands and told him that we had to go, because I sensed that they were going to come back. "There is no place to go," he said. A very high cliff enclosed the beach, and there was no way out besides the direction the men had just gone. Swimming was not an option since the currents were strong. I pointed to the cliff and told him, "We have to climb it." Jaime and I were in good shape and were also good climbers, so with our adrenaline peaking we climbed the rocks until we reached the top.

Once at the top we moved into the bushes and I said, "Please let's hide here for a moment, I know for sure that they are going to come back." And they did. We saw them down on the beach looking for us. Jaime and I held each other's hands very tightly while I prayed. The men looked up and all around, but after a few minutes they gave up and left. Jaime looked at me and asked, "How did you know that they were going to come back?"

"I don't know... I just knew," I answered, although I was sure that we had been saved by the Beings of Light.

Those mountains were very dry and covered with bushes full of thorns. All we had on were our swimsuits. When we finally reached the road we had cuts, scrapes and thorns all over our bodies, especially under our feet, but it was as if we couldn't feel any pain. We waited in the bushes until we heard a car coming, then jumped into the road waving our arms and yelling for help. The people in the car were a group of scuba divers, and when they saw us in such bad shape they stopped and picked us up. Jaime had some family members who lived close by, whom we were supposed to visit later that day, so he asked them to take us there. Thankfully, we made it safely home.

Later on, we went to the police to report the incident. Even though we were able to give a very detailed description of the three men, in the end nothing ever happened and we decided to just let it go. However, we learned from the police that we were lucky to be alive, since a few murders had been reported in the vicinity of this beach paradise.

When Jaime and I recalled the incident together, he was deeply upset thinking about how close we were to being badly harmed or killed. He couldn't understand how we were able to make it out of this nightmare, how I was able to free my hands when I was tied up, and why the men left. He had so many unresolved questions but one thing was clear to him: "I never believed in miracles before today," he said. "This was a miracle."

"We just have to be grateful because we are in God's hands," I replied. "It is clear that it wasn't our time to die... I truly believe that God wants us alive for some purpose." After a short pause, I continued: "This is not the first time that something like this has happened to me. My life has been full of miracles." Then I told Jaime about the time I almost drowned, and all the incidents when I was in great danger but came out completely unscathed. "I cannot explain to you how all this happened, but if you didn't believe in guardian angels or protective forces before, this is the time."

"I guess that we are not alone after all," he said calmly. After that day, we never talked about the incident again. Deep inside I understood that what happened had opened up Jaime somehow, and that we had become a lot closer spiritually, just as happened years before with Santiago.

On the other hand, it shook me to realize that day on the beach just for a second I sensed that I had become one with my enemy. According to the Beings of Light, if we are able to see through the veil of judgment, deep inside every experience there is a call for unity, self-love and forgiveness. So was he in reality my enemy? Or it was just a perception of my surface reality conditioned by separation? Back then this idea seemed pretty confusing and hard to grasp.

CHAPTER 29

Chaos and Doubt

DURING my second semester in Santa Marta my financial situation kept worsening, since the allowance from my dad kept changing, depending on his monthly expenses. Sometimes I had just enough to cover the rent. To make things easier I moved with other roommates to cheaper housing. The new place was nothing special, but helped make the little money I had last longer. It was farther away from the university, but since I had my bike it didn't matter. Additionally, I got a job working as a waitress in a new, fancy restaurant where I was able to make some decent tips. However, working and trying to keep up with a demanding curriculum proved to be very hard. I barely was able to sleep at night, and felt so exhausted that sometimes I had trouble performing even the most basic tasks.

In the meantime my relationship with Jaime was deteriorating rapidly, chiefly because we couldn't see each other anymore. Travelling to Santa Marta was expensive. I loved him so deeply that I knew that we could work it out despite the distance, but for him it had become too painful to bear. Jaime was a very popular and handsome man and I knew that he was always in need of attention. We didn't stop talking, but decided that it was best to keep living our own separate lives and see what happened down the road.

Although I went along with the idea, I felt totally devastated.

Breaking up with Jaime, and feeling that my dad had almost abandoned me, brought me into deep sadness. *God, I don't understand why all this hardship?* I questioned. *What is it that you want from me? I am trying to remain positive but you are making it way too hard for me.*

When my mom learned that I was depressed, she suggested that my youngest sister Fabi come to visit me. But things only seemed to worsen. She came with the very little money my mom was able to gather, so I had to keep working to sustain us both, barely having any time to be with her.

Two weeks after her arrival, one evening before going to work, a guy named Alejandro whom I'd met recently came to my place to invite me out.

"I have invited some friends to ride on my newly refurbished boat next Saturday. Would you like to come?"

"Oh! I'm sorry. I cannot go because I work on Saturdays," I answered. "By the way this is my sister," I said pointing at Fabi, standing next to me.

"Your sister must be bored with you being so busy, just take the Saturday off and bring her out. She is going to love being out there in this beautiful paradise."

"Thanks, it sounds great, I will think about it."

Once he left my sister asked who he was. I told her that I just had met him a few weeks before at the telecommunications office, while I was waiting for a telephone booth to be available to call Mom. According to him, he was new in town and didn't have phone service in his new place yet. He told me about his new boat and I also learned that he lived only a few blocks away from my apartment on the same avenue. After that day, I kept meeting him quite often while riding my bike to campus. Sometimes I would stop and chat with him for a few minutes. He was a charming and handsome guy in his mid-forties, single after divorcing his wife not long before. Due to his appearance and the expensive look of his belongings, he appeared to be in a very good shape financially. He invited me out a couple of times but I had rejected his invitations because I thought he was too old for me. I was only twenty-one.

After thinking that I wanted to spend some quality time with my sister, I decided that this time I would accept his invitation. So I took a day off from work and was able to enjoy a very fun day with her onboard a beautiful boat. Back at home my sister Fabi told me, "I know that you are not interested in dating this guy, but he really likes you... and if you think about it, he could be the solution to the miserable financial situation that you are facing right now."

"Oh my God. That sounds awful, I don't think I could do that."

"You are right, don't listen to me. I sound like the devil," she said.

We didn't talk any more about the subject for the remaining two weeks we were together. Since Alejandro knew the day of my sister's departure he came by on that morning, offering to take us to the bus station. We took his offer and went with him. After Fabi left I felt even more down and miserable than before. Other than the one day we went out with Alejandro, I couldn't do much with her.

"Would you like to go and grab something to eat?" he suggested.

"No thanks, just take me home."

"Come on, you look way too sad. Don't go home to be alone. That will just make things worse."

I accepted and he took me to a restaurant where we talked for a long time. He was a great guy and during those days when I was feeling so low he was always there to offer me his support. I liked him as a friend and although I sensed that he wanted something more, I kept my distance, thinking that he was old enough to be my father. Over time I actually started to perceive him as a father figure, and feel that way about him.

He played this role for a while, but after a few weeks it became very clear that he was not looking for a daughter. One day he invited me and other friends for a trip on his boat. At the end of the day we spotted an isolated beach and he suggested that we stop. Once there we settled on the beach to have some drinks, and then he asked me if I wanted to go for a walk with him. I agreed, feeling uneasy. While we were walking he held my hand and it was there when I realized that I had to make a decision. Feeling very nervous, I recalled the conversation I'd had with my sister and thought, *If I do this I would be betraying my beliefs about never dating somebody because I have a need... but if I don't, I am afraid that I am going to lose him.* At this point I wasn't exercising the best judgment since I was feeling so drained, so needy of love and attention, and too tired of struggling financially. *I don't want him to go*, I thought. Perhaps we could try and see what happens.

While I was thinking this, he turned toward me, gently grabbed my face and kissed me. It was the first time that I had ever kissed someone because I felt that I had to, not because I really wanted it to. It felt awkward and confusing because in my feelings I perceived him as a father rather than a lover.

After that day, he started to shower me with presents and trying to take care of my financial needs. There was nothing he wouldn't attempt to give to me or do for me. However, the more he did, the more I felt guilty and in debt, so I tried to not ask for anything. I was not sure that we should be together, so I wanted to keep living my life without needing or having too much. I thought that would make it easier for both of us if we wanted to walk away. But with him it was not possible. Soon I learned that he was used to a world in which everything could be solved with money.

He belonged to a wealthy family, and had money on his own as a pilot, flying private charters for executives over the Eastern Caribbean. Then he had moved to the Colombian Caribbean, where he was planning to buy some land and build a diving and fishing resort.

When I told my dad that I was dating Alejandro he stopped giving me any financial support, even though I shared with him my reservations about the relationship. Not having my dad's aid made the whole situation even more difficult for me. I couldn't support myself in an expensive city working part time as a waitress. Alejandro suggested that we live together but I couldn't agree, so he offered to lend me the money I needed until I could get a better job. The more supportive and closer Alejandro became, the more attached I grew, and the deeper my needy feelings became. He treated me so well that I thought that perhaps one day I would learn to love him the way he loved me. So I decided to keep trying, and take it one day at a time.

My greatest challenge began the moment we became sexually involved. Making love with my ex-boyfriend Jaime had been an amazing experience because I totally adored him, but being with someone I didn't love in the same way was emotionally challenging. I finally told Alejandro that things were not going to work and we broke up. Yet this only lasted for a few days, because he began sending me all kinds of beautiful notes and presents. I was too afraid of losing his friendship and we reunited. During those days

I felt deeply confused, doubting my values and my spirituality. *How could a person like me be considered spiritual?* I wondered. My mind became filled with negative thinking and I was very angry at myself for allowing all this to happen. But, I continued dating Alejandro anyway.

After completing three semesters in Santa Marta I was required to move to Cartagena, where I would complete my last semester of college classes. By now I had been dating Alejandro for eight months and he had become my world, especially because my contact with family and friends back home only happened by phone once in a while. Being with Alejandro was definitely a world of contrasts, because we fought a lot — something I'd never experienced before — but we also had fun together. We both loved adventure so I was able to travel, sail, ride boats, and spend countless hours under the ocean scuba diving.

At this point I felt I'd become a different person. My mind was filled with negative thinking. I began to lose sleep and started to have nightmares about the times of neglect and abuse I experienced during my childhood. I usually felt disappointed, angry and moody. I felt so much guilt and shame within myself that I thought that I wasn't deserving of the Beings of Light. To distance myself from them I stopped praying and meditating. That worked. Eventually, I couldn't feel their presence anymore.

CHAPTER 30

Beauty is in the Heart

WHEN IT was time to move to Cartagena I didn't want to carry much. Since we had a car, I realized that I wasn't going to need the bike that the beach boy gave me anymore. Then I remembered the message attached to the bike, about letting it go when I didn't need it. When I started to wonder about where I should leave the bike, the answer came quickly.

The last day of classes, the cleaning lady who worked for us told me that while I was at school a very charming guy had come by and told her that I could leave the bike parked at the front gate. He would come and pick it up later. Then I looked up at the sky thinking, *So he knows where I live!* By then I had moved twice since I met him. However, I had been hoping to meet him again so I could thank him personally.

"When is he coming to get it?" I asked the maid, feeling overjoyed.

"He said not to worry because he will not be back before you leave town," she answered. Tears of happiness rolled down my cheeks as thoughts of the Beings of Light immediately filled my mind; *Somehow, I know that you have something to do with this.* Then I thanked and hugged the cleaning lady.

Before leaving town I left the bike where I was told with a note saying: *"Thank you so much for the bike. With this gift you brought joy into my life. I wish I could have seen you again. Wishing you the best, Ingrid."*

Once I moved to Cartagena, I thought about living with my classmates but Alejandro surprised me by renting an apartment just for me. Since he was still living in Santa Marta he said, "Please take it, that way when I come visit we can stay together." I agreed. But I didn't live alone for too long because he decided to move to Cartagena, and then we ended up living together. I wasn't happy with the idea, and we began to fight more often.

Cartagena is a beautiful and busy city, visited by thousands of tourists from all over the world. The campus there was also bigger, so I started to meet lots of new people. All this made Alejandro feel insecure and he became very possessive, to the point of wanting to take me and pick me up from wherever I went. To make matters worse, halfway through the semester I was chosen, along with my friend Johanna, by the Faculty of Marine Biology, to participate in an annual contest put on by the university. In this contest, the most charming girl of the whole campus would be named and crowned.

I felt surprised and honored when I learned that my classmates had chosen me. At the beginning I was hesitant, but as the event progressed I got to meet some amazing girls and had a lot of fun along the way. I actually loved the whole experience, since the contest was about finding inner beauty. Some of the girls weren't very attractive physically, but they were extremely charming and conducted themselves with self-confidence, making them all extremely lovable.

On the day of the coronation, my classmates and I were ecstatic when I was picked by the judges as the second most charming girl of the whole campus. During this experience I gained so much confidence, because I was finally able to realize that real beauty was within. Growing up, when I used to complain about my looks to the Beings of Light they would say, "True beauty is in the heart. The world of the form is not permanent and someday the physical aspect of your body will deteriorate, but the wonderful thing is that the inner beauty will never fade." But back in those days I didn't want to listen. I just wanted to be as pretty as my sisters were.

Due to the contest I gained so much popularity that Alejandro became even more controlling and jealous. We argued almost constantly. He was able to awaken in me the most aggressive behavior that I had ever manifested. My family and friends always used to remark about how much it would take for me to get angry. But when I was with Alejandro, sometimes I felt like a monster. At this point in the relationship I felt trapped, because I felt that I loved him for all the good things he had done for me, but I also wanted to run. I literally felt that I couldn't live with this guy — but also couldn't live without him.

He also had a very explosive temper and could become very aggressive at times. One day he almost beat me in public, during a friend's house party, because he was furious at me for talking to another guy. As he grabbed and pulled my hair, twisting my head back with his other hand lifted ready to strike my face, one of his cousins intervened, yelling, "Stop, she isn't saying or doing anything inappropriate. Are you insane?" After this incident, as he had done in the past, Alejandro would ask for forgiveness with tears in his eyes. Because I was so afraid of being without him, we made up again.

Yet after this episode I'd had enough. I was ready to leave him but had to find the courage. "Beings of Light, I haven't asked for your help for a while because I haven't felt deserving, but please help me find the courage I need to leave. I know this is madness but I feel so afraid of being without him, I am surrounded by many people, but without you I feel so lonely," I prayed.

A few days later I was floored when I met the beach boy once again! It was a very fast encounter that happened while we were waiting for a traffic light to turn green. I was sitting in the passenger's seat of Alejandro's car when I turned my head to the right, hearing loud music, and there he was, driving the car next to us. Quickly I rolled my window down and almost flung my body out of the car window.

"Hey Ingrid!" he yelled with a huge smile when he saw me.

I expressed to him all my gratitude about the bike and he said that it was nothing. I asked, "Where have you been? What are you doing here in Cartagena?"

"I am living here in an apartment located in the old town."

"Let's meet again!" I shouted.

But at that moment the traffic light changed and everyone's horns went off. It was a very busy avenue so he just yelled, "Don't worry. I am sure we will meet again." Then we waved and smiled at each other.

I hadn't been this excited to see someone for so long. Looking very upset, Alejandro asked me who the guy was, and I told him that he was a friend whom I hadn't seen for quite a long time. I told Alejandro that I met him in Santa Marta long before we started to date, and that I never expected to meet him again after moving to a new city.

"Wow, what are the odds of that?" he said.

"Yes, what are the odds of that!" I answered, while thinking that "odds" or "coincidences" didn't exist in the world of the Beings of Light. After that day, I never saw him again but I was very grateful because the Beings of Light had given me the opportunity to see him one last time. They also made me feel certain that meeting this guy had been their doing from the very beginning. Once more it became clear to me that I wasn't on my own, and everything happened for a reason.

When I was younger the Beings of Light once said to me, "The moment that you think that you are alone, close your eyes and you will see from within that loneliness does not exist."

I might never know who the guy I met at the beach truly was, but it didn't matter; the important thing was that we were put on each other's path for a good reason. I don't know what I possibly meant to him, but I met him at some crucial moments in my life when I needed him the most. That is, I needed a strong reminder that I was not alone.

The last encounter with the beach boy brought me to understand that the Beings of Light had never left, and this gave me the courage I had asked for. So I made my final decision to leave Alejandro. To avoid more conflict or violence I didn't mention my true intentions to him. Since I already had a trip to Bogota planned to visit family and friends at the end of the semester, when the time came, I packed a few things and left with the idea of never to come back.

CHAPTER 31

Scarcity, a Trick of the Limited Mind

L EARNING that the Beings of Light had always been with me despite my behavior gave me a glimpse into the meaning of love and compassion. Clearly, they were not here to judge me. Trying to follow their example, I talked to my dad and decided to forgive whatever misfortunes had happened in the past. I made peace with everyone at home, including my dad's lover who had been living with him for the past couple of years.

By this time, I had finished with all my classes and received an offer to go to an island in the Caribbean, San Andres, where I would work with my classmate Johanna on a thesis about mangrove ecosystems. While acquiring my undergraduate diploma as a Marine Biologist, it was necessary in Colombia to do a thesis to graduate from the program. After spending a couple weeks in Bogota, I accepted the offer and moved to the island.

Meanwhile, Alejandro had been looking incessantly for me, but I avoided all his calls. Once on the island Johanna and I moved in together into one small bedroom that we rented in someone else's apartment. We were not going to make much money working with this project, so this way we could make the money last longer. Although I was trying not to feel discouraged I thought, *Only a couple of months ago I was living like a queen and now I am back to counting coins again...*

As the weeks passed I started to think more and more about Alejandro. I knew for a fact that I was better without him but I had become too attached. He was like an addictive drug and although I knew that calling him back would be a huge mistake, one day I couldn't resist the impulse anymore. I grabbed the phone and called him back. He was so happy to hear from me that the same day he filled my bank account with money — and the very next day he flew to the island. When we saw each other we hugged and kissed as if we haven't seen each other for years. I thought that maybe this time things could be different.

Since he wasn't going to move to the island because his new diving business was settling in Cartagena, he rented a gorgeous apartment overlooking the ocean for me to live in with Johanna. I thought that by seeing each other less we could work out our differences. But he still wanted to manage my life. At the time there were no cellphones yet on the island, so he would call the apartment's phone constantly. Out of frustration and anger we would have huge arguments over the phone. His visits were no better, since there was always something that would bring us to quarrel.

We kept living in this endless drama for almost another year. One night during one of his visits, I told him, "It is clear that things with us are not working."

"What do you mean, do you want to break up with me? Is that what you want?" he yelled in anger.

"Maybe that's what is best for us," I replied very nervously.

By talking to him this way I knew that I was facing one of my biggest fears: reprisal and punishment. Deep within I had carried these emotions with me since I was little. The first time I left Alejandro I didn't face him and just ran away because of these anxieties.

He became so angry with me that he quickly transformed into a beast, pacing around the apartment while screaming all kinds of hurtful things. He reminded me that he had given me all the things I had, as he always did, then added, "Don't think that you are so special. I could have chosen someone else... As a matter of fact when I met you at the telephone service office, it was almost a tie between you and one of your classmates." I was speechless. Then he pulled a knife out of his pocket and went into the bedroom, where he proceeded to cut up my clothes.

Listening to the blade ripping the clothes apart, I remained seated in the living room completely petrified. I had never seen him this angry. As he was cutting one of my boots he sliced his hand. He screamed so loud and when he came out of the bedroom bleeding, I tried to run towards the front door to leave the apartment. He reached the door first and locked the bolt, taking the key. I was living in a sixth floor apartment, but when I found myself totally cornered I didn't care about anything anymore. I ran to the balcony, and jumped. Alejandro was running behind me so he was able to catch one of my legs and pull me back into the apartment. I hit my body hard against the building wall, scraping one arm and part of my face. After he pulled me back he held me in his arms, he started to cry and ask for forgiveness.

That night I realized that we definitely had gone too far, but to stop the situation from getting even worse, I gave in and accepted his apology. While Alejandro was still sleep, at morning's first light I sneaked out of the apartment, took an ATV he had given me and drove far away to an isolated beach to be able to think and ask for guidance. "I thought that things were really going to be better between us, but I was wrong." I cried to the Beings of Light. "I want to erase it all and forget that all this ever happened. I wish I never

met him... It is clear that nothing matters if all I want is to die,"
I wept.

As I started to calm down an old memory popped into my
mind, about a time when I had to face a moment of terror. It had
happened about a year earlier during one of our extreme scuba
diving experiences. The plan was to dive into a very narrow cave
starting from the entrance at about 100 feet down, exiting ten feet
from the surface. We were diving at night during a full moon, so
when we went into the water it was beautiful to see the moon
from underneath the water. I knew that the cave was narrow but I
didn't know how narrow it was until I entered it. Only one person
could fit at a time. Two divers were at the front, then me, and
then Alejandro was last. We were moving very slowly and as we
advanced a few feet into the cave, suddenly I had a dreadful feeling
of being trapped. An enormous terror took over my mind and my
body, bringing back the past life memory where I had died as a
prisoner in a hole in the ground.

I could feel my heart beating faster and losing control of all
my senses while shaking uncontrollably. Suddenly I saw myself
talking to me as if I was reflected in a mirror: "There is nothing to
fear. You can do this. The fear is only in your mind." Right then I
saw a red fish with a big round eye coming out from a crevice,
moving very slowly into the flashlight's beam, distracting me for
a second.

"See, you were able to shift your mind from the fear to the
fish, and for a second you were able to forget all about the fear. It
is your decision to cross this cave, and even enjoy it, or stay here
in fear."

Then I took control of my body, breathing deep through the
regulator and slowly starting to move while more fish started to

appear. Soon I was enjoying the moment, and forgetting everything about the fear.

So that day at the beach, I clearly understood that nothing good could come from a fearful mind. It was up to me to leave Alejandro and free myself from all this pain. *I know that if I release all attachments I can be free*, I thought, with the Beings of Light in mind. "Thank you for opening my mind and never leaving my side," I said to them.

Since I was working with the Wildlife Department of Conservation where I had made new friends over the past year, I drove the ATV to the agency and asked one of my friends if he could come with me in his vehicle. That way I could drop the ATV off safely at the apartment complex. Then I walked away with only the clothes on my back, leaving absolutely everything else behind.

Later in the day I talked to Alejandro by phone and told him that I wasn't coming. He was furious and tried to scare me with all kinds of threatening messages, which only reinforced the fact that we were done. Thankfully, I had been able to make some very good friends who knew my situation with Alejandro, they were there to protect me and give me a hand when I needed it. The last time I talked to him on my office phone he yelled, "I am going to throw all your stuff in the trash."

"Do it. I am okay with it, I don't need it anymore. I have my life and that is all I need to start again," I firmly replied. Then I never answered his calls at the office again. He thought that everything could be solved with money and he wasn't used to hearing *"No"* for an answer. During those days it was definitely proven to me that money couldn't buy happiness, and that anger and fear were very destructive forces when held permanently in the heart.

He thought I was going to come back as I had done before, but I never did. According to him I was losing everything, but according to me I was winning it all. The moment I walked away from this relationship of almost three years I recognized that as long as I had the Beings of Light and myself, I had everything I needed. Feeling grateful for this eliminated any fear I had of lacking anything.

And the more I was willing to let go of the fear of lack, the more I received. I got love and support from those I knew and a few I didn't, finding immediate shelter and food at every table. I even got a huge increase in salary, because I was hired to work on a big government contract as the lead scientist for a Nationwide Mangrove Project. So not long after the breakup, at twenty-four, I had everything I needed to live a comfortable life. I wasn't living in a palace but I felt so loved, free and grateful that I found myself living in paradise.

Once the Beings of Light said to me, "Everything one has now is everything one needs." Only after this experience did I finally understand this teaching. The right circumstances are ready for us when we become ready for them. I just had to become aware of the fact that lack and limitation were concepts of the limited mind. I also realized that nothing is ever given or taken away from us, because nothing belongs to anybody.

After this experience, I also became more compassionate, realizing that I never know the reasons that have moved somebody to do what they do. When I was very young I remember listening to a conversation between a few young girls when one of them said, "Someday when I grow older, I wish to marry a rich man so I can have a comfortable and happy life." The rest of the girls agreed with her. I remember feeling so repulsed and thinking, *I would never wish for something like that. How stupid to think that way* — yet there I had been, doing what I had judged others for just talking about. Without the struggle with Alejandro, I would never have developed a deeper compassion.

CHAPTER 32

No Need to Worry

I LANDED my first big job about two months after I broke up with Alejandro. I was still living on San Andres Island, and working on my thesis. My advisor Martha was called by the Ministry of Environment of Colombia to work for one year on a nationwide project on mangrove ecosystems. This was a very robust project funded by the Colombia, UNESCO, and the Japanese government. However, she rejected the offer because she already had accepted another one abroad. Thus she asked me if I would be willing to take this job instead of her. "Come with me to the headquarters of the Ministry of Environment in Bogota. The project will pay for the airplane tickets and you can accompany me to the interview," she offered.

Once there, she introduced me to the director. They chatted for a while and at the end of the conversation he said, "Martha, I trust your judgment about Ingrid. If you have chosen her, it is because you know she can do the job." He then turned to me and asked: "Are you ready to assume the leadership of this project?" As he was looking directly into my eyes I felt the sense that I already knew him. Just like that I felt completely peaceful and confident to say: "Yes, I can do it."

For the next year, the island became my paradise and my

experience working on the mangrove project was a total success, for which I received other job offers. However, as this commitment ended, I felt the yearning for a change. This desire came right after a motorcycle accident, on the first day I ever tried to ride one. As I was just getting comfortable with riding on flat surfaces, a friend of mine asked me to take him to a neighborhood that was located up a steep hill. It was night and I didn't know what I was doing, so I was tense and hesitant. Finally I agreed, but while changing gears, something happened and suddenly we were on the ground. Other than a few scrapes my friend was okay, but my head hit the ground very hard, and I wasn't wearing a helmet.

I stood up feeling nothing — no pain, no fear, no emotions whatsoever. I was fully aware that I wanted to leave my human experience and join the Beings of Light. A passerby offered to carry me to the hospital; at that moment I realized that I could hear the voice of this person, but I couldn't see him. My eyes were open but I couldn't see, and an extreme sense of panic took over my entire being when I realized that I was blind. It took about one hour to recover my vision. While at the hospital the doctor told me that I must have lost my vision when my head hit the ground. I looked at my friend and said, "I don't think I could have been blind when I hit the ground because I saw all the lights around us when I stood up."

My friend answered, "Ingrid, where the accident happened it was pitch-black." After a pause he said, "By the way, you never stood up after the accident."

Then I realized that I'd had a brief out-of-body experience, and I had seen the lights with the eyes of my soul. Despite everything, I felt very excited because I sensed that the lights had to belong to the Beings of Light, whom I had not seen for almost five years.

While healing from the accident, many thoughts and memories

came to my mind — among them the persistent impression that I already knew the director of the mangrove project, before we were introduced. Then I clearly remembered I had met him during the vision I had while walking on the street with my mom, when I was twelve. He was one of the highly educated people sitting at a desk in the office, looking at me while sharing his knowledge.

After this last revelation I felt there was more I had to do beyond the limits of this island. A good friend of mine told me that she had joined a program where she had spent a year in France learning the language, and had the opportunity to travel around Europe. I'd always dreamed about going to Europe, and this program sounded like the perfect opportunity.

While contemplating this move, another memory came to my mind. It was a day on which Alejandro and I went diving into a shipwreck with a group of divers. It was a big cargo ship that had sunk off the coast of the Colombian Caribbean years before. On a bright sunny day around mid-morning we went into the water to a depth of about 100 feet. Inside the ship we all turned on our flashlights because the interior corridors were in complete darkness. We had to move slowly using the hand railings, because any strong movement could disturb the deposits of thin sediment causing the water to become cloudy, obscuring visibility.

After visiting a few dark confined spaces where I needed to point my flashlight directly at what I wanted to see to guide myself, we finally reached a vast open area. As soon as we dove into this room I saw one of the most amazing sights I had ever seen in nature. There was an intense beam of radiant blue light descending like a waterfall through a porthole located at the top of this huge room. Seeing the beauty of this luminous beam after being in the dark was something quite majestic. The first thing I did was to dive directly into the light. I felt as if I wanted to be bathed by this magnificent light and when I turned around, I saw the rest of the divers in the light as well. Everyone was moving their arms, as if to embrace the light.

One of the most amazing things about diving is the absence of expression through voice; it is a time when you can feel deep joy with a group of people without the need for words. After being in the light I thought, *There is no way I am going back into the darkness; the only way I would leave this ship is by diving through that porthole.* Then the leader of the group pointed at the porthole and gave us the sign to go through it. I thought, *Wow, this beautiful blue light is an extension of the light coming from the ocean.* Once through the porthole, moving towards the surface, I thought, *Wow the light of the ocean comes from the most powerful source, the sun.* I was caught completely by surprise when I heard, "And the sun is an extension of *That* which embraces all."

Recalling this reconnection with the Beings of Light, it became clear to me that there was so much more to learn that I decided to leave the island, and join the program to go to Europe.

After being accepted into the program to study French for one year in the Université Catholique D'Angers, I started to organize my finances and sell everything I had bought during the past year. With that plus the money I had saved working on the mangrove project I had enough to survive for about half a year in France. To be able to cover the remaining year I was planning to look for a loan and perhaps ask my family for help, since they were doing a lot better financially.

One evening while walking on the beach and dreaming about the trip I ran into a big surprise. It was my ex Alejandro, whom I hadn't seen in over a year. Although San Andres was a small island, all this time I had been able to avoid seeing him. When I saw him, I felt both astonishment and worry. If I could I would have hidden, but we met right on a wide, open beach. He was staying at a very beautiful hotel and was just stepping out to see the sunset.

He was extremely excited to see me. "I have been doing some business here on the island and every time I'm here I'm always hoping to see you again," he exclaimed. Despite everything, he had played a very important role in my life so I felt touched by his intense reaction. I wanted to leave quickly, but as always, he used his charm to convince me to stay. "Please don't go, let's just talk for a little while," he pleaded.

So we sat at one of the tables at the beach-bar, where I felt more comfortable surrounded by people. We talked a little about family and work, and then I told him that I was ready to leave the island to go to Europe. He became quiet and looked at me, half-smiling.

Next, he fixed his attention on a small bump I had on my forehead as a result of my motorcycle accident. In a very gentle way he touched my forehead and looked at me with watery eyes saying, "You don't imagine how much I have missed you and how much I regret the way our relationship ended." I was speechless. He continued talking, "Since you left I have been haunted by the sad memories of the awful way I treated you at the end, and the way you left with only the clothes on your back... I never imagined that you would ever leave me."

I remained completely still and quiet; bringing back all these memories was painful. He continued talking about how every day he thought about me and prayed for my well-being. He said that he felt guilty for any difficult moments I'd faced during the previous year, including the accident that led to the bump on my forehead. He knew how fascinated I always had been about Europe. So after becoming silent for a moment he continued saying, "I know how much you have dreamed about going to Europe, and I would rather beg for you to stay but I know that I have lost you."

At this point I didn't even know what to feel or how to react. So I just replied, "You don't have to worry, I am fine. Life has treated me well."

"Sorry I don't mean to interrupt, but I have to make a quick phone call," Alejandro said. "I have a business dinner tonight and I need to say that I am going to be a little bit late."

"It is okay, I also need to go."

"Please stay for a little longer I will be right back," he insisted. Then he turned to one of the hotel security guards and yelled at him, "If she tries to leave you let me know." He smiled as if it was a joke, but I knew it wasn't.

It took him a little while to come back and when he returned he was holding something in his hand. He sat at the table and said, "I know that you just told me that you are doing okay and that your trip to Europe is all set, but I want to compensate somehow for the harm I have caused to you. I want you to have the best time in Europe, so please accept this gift from me." He handed me an envelope full of money.

"I cannot take it," I responded, giving it back to him. I was immediately afraid that he wanted to use money to manipulate me.

"It is getting late and I have to go," he replied. Then he stood up and whispered in my ear, "Think about it tonight and if you don't want it bring it back to me tomorrow." He left the envelope on the table.

"There is nothing to think about," I asserted, trying to hand it back but he held his hands up, refusing. He looked at me with a smile and then walked away.

As he was walking away his aura was shining bright, which made me feel that his intentions were honest. So I grabbed the money and went home. Once there I counted the money, and to my surprise there was more than I ever asked for during all my prayers. I was praying for a few coins and instead I hit the jackpot. That night I couldn't sleep, and kept asking for guidance from the Beings of Light. Then suddenly I heard, "Take what is being offered to you. This is meant to help you both."

Although I didn't understand the full meaning of this message at the time, it became clear to me that the meeting with Alejandro had not been coincidental. So I followed the guidance, feeling grateful for this heavenly gift.

Alejandro was not the only one feeling guilty, since I always had held similar feelings within myself about the whole relationship. That night I decided to write him a little thank-you note. The next morning I went back to the hotel, handing the note to the receptionist to be forwarded. She replied, "Sorry, but Mr. Alejandro left the island early this morning." Then she asked me my name and handed me a note in return where he had written:

"Seeing you again was the best thing that had happened to me in a very long time. I don't expect you to forgive me but I hope that you don't hate me. I only ask you for one thing, and that is to please call me if you ever need anything. Enjoy Europe. I love you, Alejandro."

Right there I sensed an intense feeling of love and compassion for both of us, and the resentment I was holding against him faded away.

I told all my friends on the island that I was going to come back once the program in Europe was over. However, the day I left the island, while sitting on the airplane the Beings of Light revealed: "You are not going to come back, your experience here has ended."

I shed some tears of sadness, but at the same time I felt happy because I realized that a whole world of new experiences was waiting for me.

CHAPTER 33

We Are Where We Have to Be

IN JUNE 1996 at the age of twenty-five, I graduated as a Marine
Biologist in Bogota, where I spent two months enjoying the
company of my family and my friends Santiago and Angelica.
Arriving thereafter in Europe was like stepping into another world.
Something I had considered almost unreachable when I was younger had become real. The first night while resting at the college
dormitory in Angers, France, I felt so much gratitude to the Beings
of Light, for teaching me once again that nothing was impossible.
The only limits were the obstacles within my own mind.

After six months studying French at the University of Angers I
started to feel an intense push to leave the program. Once I learned
French, which happened easily and effortlessly, I couldn't stop an
intense urge to learn English. After much consideration I left the
program a few months before it ended. This decision didn't sit well
with the university but in the end all was resolved and I was re-
funded part of my tuition.

While still living in France I had learned that a Colombian
friend was living in Edinburgh, Scotland. After asking him by phone
where I might find a school to learn English, he offered his apartment until I could find a place to live. With his help I found two
small colleges where I soon enrolled to learn English. After about

a month living in Edinburgh, I met a very interesting British man named Tom at a dinner party.

He was a very tall, good-looking guy with blue eyes, long blonde hair and a slim, but strong physique. I didn't talk much at the dinner table because I was just learning to speak the language, and it was very hard for me to understand most of what was being said due to the heavy Scottish accents, except for Tom. At times my head was so tired trying to process all the words that I could hear only noise, but Tom had such a poised and clear British accent that every time he spoke his words sounded like music to my ears.

A couple of times he caught me staring at him, and he would look directly into my eyes with a very serious expression and then smile. It felt like I had some kind of connection with him, but I didn't know what to make of it so I decided to keep my distance and stop looking at him. After dinner we all went to a going-away party at someone else's house. Once there, Tom and I happened to sit next to each other, and engaged in an extended conversation for the rest of the night. I don't know how we did it, but we managed to understand each other. We also laughed a lot when we couldn't get our points across. He said that this was the first time in months that he had felt so comfortable and content since he had returned to Scotland.

We were soon dating, and I learned that after working for a few years with the Wild World Foundation in Indonesia and Australia, he had been forced to return to Scotland because his mother had fallen ill and he wanted to be closer to her. Since his return, his life had been miserable because he didn't get along with his father, and he was living on government welfare as he hadn't been able to find a job. This situation made him very angry and depressed, which explained why his aura looked rather dim the day I met him.

Not long after we started to date he said to me, "I want to make things clear to you... don't take it wrong, but I am not ready for a commitment." Since my English vocabulary wasn't too rich I just looked at him and asked,

"What does a commitment mean?"

As he struggled to find a way to explain, he finally smiled and said, "Let's just forget about it and concentrate on having fun."

"Okay that sounds better to me," I replied.

During those days I wasn't interested in having any drama and although I learned later what "commitment" meant, I just let it go and kept having fun.

Tom was a spiritual person with a huge urge for freedom, so in that sense we were very similar. However, when we met he had been trapped for almost two years in a situation that made him feel incapable of moving on. He didn't want to live in Scotland, but he also didn't want to leave his mom behind while she was still sick. He was sharing an apartment with two other people, but he was afraid that one day he wouldn't be able to pay the rent and would end up homeless. Nevertheless, Tom said that I had brought light into his life.

At this point I still had money, but living in France had been more expensive than I anticipated. To be safe I got a job cleaning and organizing furniture in a store for two days a week. I tried not to worry since, after all, my stay in Europe was only a vacation that would end soon. *Enjoy the moment*, I repeated to myself.

Tom would also take on little jobs here and there to earn money. When we were not busy trying to find the means to survive we would spend our time together walking in the park, meditating, reading, talking and meeting friends. As my ability to speak English improved, we would find ourselves in deep spiritual conversations.

Although Tom didn't want a commitment in the beginning, after four months he felt so close to me that he decided it was time for me to meet his family. This was surprising because he barely talked about them except for his mom. Over time I learned that his dad was a scientist, whom he considered a bully, and his only brother was an engineer.

One Friday evening, we took the train to San Andrews to meet his parents. On the way there, I felt tense thinking about his father, so I closed my eyes for a while and meditated about them being at peace with each other while evoking the loving energy of the Beings of Light. Finally, when we made it all the way to his parents' house I thought that I was dreaming, for we entered an exquisite neighborhood and stopped in front of a huge, absolutely stunning house. I was shocked; I couldn't understand how Tom was going through such a rough financial situation while his parents were doing so well.

His situation made me feel sad because it reminded me of having felt abandoned by my father. Later that weekend when I asked Tom about the issue, he said to me that he didn't want anything from his father and he could survive on his own. The last thing he wanted was to show any weakness in front of his dad. But his parents were excited to meet me and treated me kindly. It was very rare that Tom would share his personal life, especially with his father.

After that lovely weekend we went to visit his parents many other times and although there was animosity between Tom and his dad, he said that all of those feelings seemed to vanish when I was around. I also went to meet his grandmother, a very proper British woman, with whom I immediately connected. She told me all the history of their very well-known and prestigious family, that had occupied very important positions in British society and government throughout history, including the present time. I found all of this truly fascinating and couldn't hide my excitement. According to Tom his family adored me, and I could certainly feel the love.

Tom's mother and I created a very special bond, partly because I was able to convince Tom to organize his bedroom — which looked more like a storage room because it was filled with boxes full of souvenirs that Tom had collected around the world. During my first visit I could see how much this bedroom meant to Tom's mother, so for a while I meditated on the best way to convince Tom to fix it up. Somehow I knew that putting this room together would bring a very positive outcome.

It took me more than a few words to convince Tom, who was very hesitant, but in the end the result was stunning. He had collected so many beautiful treasures throughout his years of travelling that we were able to transform the room into a gorgeous retreat. When we opened the door to surprise his mother she was stunned, and tears of joy streamed from her eyes. She cried not just because of the bedroom, but because she saw that Tom's life was also positively changing. Many times she expressed her gratitude to me and I always answered, "Thank you, for allowing me into the heart of your home." It was amazing to realize how something so superfluous could bring a big deal of positive change.

Almost one year had passed since Tom and I met. We loved each other deeply but my situation in Scotland had become difficult; I was running out of money and as a tourist I couldn't get a well-paying job. My visa was about to expire and there was no way for me to renew it unless I had a very good excuse for doing so. One day I asked Tom, "What would you think if we get married?"

"No!" he snapped. "We are not going to marry because we

have to, and anyway I would think that you were using me."

I didn't expect such a strong reaction from him. "It's okay, don't be mad," I said, feeling awful. "It was just a silly suggestion."

So I didn't mention the subject ever again. This was the first and only time that Tom ever talked to me that way. As the days passed, thinking about the situation and asking the Beings of Light for some clarity, I eventually recognized that Tom was right to think that way. He hadn't meant to hurt me, but I sensed that it was time for me to go.

One evening, while meditating on my own at Tom's apartment, I perceived the very bright white light of a Being of Light flooding the entire bedroom. As I was overjoyed by his presence I heard him say, "Tom and you have been helping each other throughout many different lives. Remember, time and space don't matter, so wherever you are you will meet because you have made the agreement to help each other."

"Did I also make this agreement with Jaime and Alejandro?" I asked feeling amazed and curious.

"That's right," it affirmed, and then proceeded to show me other lives in which I had encountered them, as well as members of my family. Feeling absolutely ecstatic because I hadn't connected with the Beings of Light in such a way for almost ten years, I kept asking:

"But if I am with Tom, why do I feel the urge to leave Europe?"

"You are ready for more and what is out there is ready for you. You are going to meet again with someone else back in Colombia, soon."

As the Being of Light was talking, I had a vision of meeting and marrying Daniel, someone I had met via my sister Lis when she was doing pre-med in college. Although I always thought that he was a very charming guy, we never got too close. *But how??* I thought. *I haven't seen Daniel for more than eight years!* I didn't even know if he was still a friend of my sister's. *Why him?*

"Because you are ready for each other," the Being responded.

Suddenly I was distracted by a vision of a little girl running and giggling in the distance. "Who is she?" I asked.

"Your daughter Ana," it answered.

"A daughter? I thought that I was going to have a boy?" During my teenage years I'd had a vision of a little boy, whom the Beings of Light said would be my son.

"Wow, all of this is waiting for me in the future? And what about Tom? I can't just leave him."

"There is much waiting for him too. There will be challenges but don't worry, he will be alright. You are not leaving him, you are just moving on."

Although I tried to prolong my stay in Scotland a little longer, things simply didn't work. I ran out of money and spent the last couple of months eating very little and enduring a very harsh, cold winter. When I finally decided to leave I felt sad and guilty because I couldn't tell Tom what I had learned from the Beings of Light. So the last days we spent together I shared with him every bit of my love.

By the time I left, Tom's depression was gone, his energy was radiant, and he had even gotten a job. His relationship with his father had greatly improved, to the point that after I left he was able to move into his parents' house for a couple of months until his finances had recovered. His mother's health improved as well, so in the end he ended up leaving Scotland and going back to do what he loved the most: being with nature, exploring other cultures, and being free. We missed each other deeply and kept talking for a while. Though I knew that we would remain forever-joined in spirit, we would not meet again in person.

During those days I was just beginning to grasp that there is a great purpose in all our paths, that transcends the needs of the ego.

CHAPTER 34

A Gift from the Beings of Light

DURING the time I had lived in France, I spent a couple of weeks in Paris before going to Edinburgh. While in Paris I had left some luggage at a friend's house, so before leaving Europe I had to stop at her place to pick up my bag. From her house to the Paris airport I took the train. Feeling sad and worried about Tom, I was distracted looking through the window, when a man walked into the train car where I was sitting alone. As he started to walk toward me, I immediately sensed his bad intentions.

"Speak to him in Spanish," I heard the Beings of Light say. I had no idea of the stranger's nationality, but I followed the guidance without question.

"*Hola, como estas?* (Hi, how are you doing?)," I instantly asked.

Suddenly his energy shifted from that of a predator to a relaxed human being. He stood in front of me and said with a smile, "Hey, *hermana latina* (Hey, Latino sister)." Then he asked me where I was going.

"*De regreso a casa en Colombia* (Back home to Colombia)."

"*Chevere, yo amo Colombia* (Great, I love Colombia)." After a pause he exclaimed, "*Hermana Colombiana, hoy es su día de surte* (Colombian sister, today is your lucky day)!" As soon as the train stopped, he jumped off and ran away.

For me there was no doubt that the Beings of Light were always watching over me and guiding me where I needed to go, but I
just had to learn to let go and trust. *Why has letting go been so hard?*
I thought.

After visiting France I also spent a couple of weeks in San-
tander, Spain where I wanted to say goodbye to some old friends,
Sonia and Pablo. I also needed to finish reviewing a natural history
book, authored by a woman named Marian who was the director
of a small publishing house. When I met her, I told her that I
had written a few science articles and a book about mangrove
ecosystems, and she asked me if I was interested in doing the first
edit of her book. Since I was only visiting Spain, I took all the drafts
with me and continued working while I was living in Scotland.

My friends' house was located in the countryside at the top of
a mountain where the views were absolutely breathtaking. Every
evening before my departure to Colombia, I would sit on the porch
feeling melancholy about Tom and anxious because I didn't know
what I was going to do in Colombia. I knew that I needed to trust
the Beings of Light, but I couldn't help it. I didn't have money, a
place to live, or a job. To make matters worse, one evening while
meditating on the porch I had a vision about my friends, Sonia and
Pablo, getting divorced. They had dated for years but only recently
married. I learned that he was going to leave her after meeting
someone else.

"Nothing is permanent for anyone," the Beings of Light said.
In fact their marriage did end a year later.

On the last day I spent at their house I went for a walk. While
walking around the surrounding area I encountered a path made
of gravel. Once in a friend's office in Colombia, I saw a perfectly
shaped spherical rock sitting on her desk. When I asked her about

the rock she said that it was shaped naturally and that her father had found it while walking around a creek in the mountains. It just amazed me how nature could create such a beautiful thing, so I always kept my mind on the possibility of finding a rock that looked like that.

As the day was turning dark I decided to head back to the house where my friends were fixing dinner. That night we chatted for a little while and when I went to bed I was still feeling sad and worried.

The bedroom where I was sleeping had a big window with no glass and two wooden shutters. The window ledge was low and wide so that night I sat on it to look at the stars, then closed and locked the shutters before going to bed. With the lights out, the room was so dark that I couldn't see my hands. The house was in complete silence, which I found extremely relaxing. So in that quiet and peaceful darkness I sat on the bed and tried to meditate, but my mind couldn't stop wondering about the future.

Suddenly I perceived a light flashing, and when I opened my eyes many more lights started to appear. I had seen the brightness of the Beings of Light shining many times throughout my life; however, this was like nothing I had ever seen before. The lights were in different sizes, though none bigger than a quarter, and the variety of colors was simply stunning. They were moving very fast, swirling around the whole bedroom until they were grouped altogether next to the window. Even though the scene was splendid, I had never seen the Beings of Light shining this way. I jumped out of bed and turned on the light. Finding the switch was easy because the whole room was illuminated. Then the lights were gone.

I stood next to the bed with the light on for a little while, trying to understand what had happened. Then I sensed the presence of the Beings of Light.

"Is this you trying to cheer me up?" I asked. So I turned off the light and went back to bed where I remained awake for a while, watching for something else to happen, but since nothing did I went to sleep feeling thankful. The next morning I woke up feeling better. I got up and went directly to the window to open the shutters to allow some sunlight and breeze into the room. Once the shutters were opened I looked down and discovered a little spherical rock on the window ledge. I picked it up, clenching it directly to my chest. "Everything will be alright," the Beings of Light whispered. That day I finally let go and simply stopped worrying about the future. I realized that I didn't need to waste any energy trying to find what was already waiting for me. I didn't need to find the rock anymore, because it found me. Although I still didn't know how things were going to go for me in Colombia, I went back with the most precious gift, a heart full of gratitude, and an open mind at ease.

CHAPTER 35

Ana

BY APRIL of 1998 I was back in Bogota, Colombia at my mom's house until I could find a job. The very first day, I asked my sister Lis if she knew anything about Daniel, as these thoughts had been haunting me since the day I learned that we were to meet again. My sister said that she had not seen him for years and thought by now he must be married. The last time they ran into each other, he was engaged.

"Why are you asking about him?" Lis wondered.

"Oh, no special reason. I just dreamt about him recently, which brought me to remember our early years of college and all the fun we had partying together."

"Yes, it was a great time. After I switched majors I lost connection with almost everyone from the pre-med program. I didn't keep any contact information."

"I imagine Daniel is busy being a doctor," I mused.

"I bet! But even if he remembers us, we have moved a few times and changed phone numbers, so how could he even find us," Lis stated.

That night I wondered how Daniel and I were going to meet in a city of ten million people. But then thought, *If the Beings of Light said so, it is going to happen.* Then I just let it go. Four weeks later the telephone rang at my mom's house, and it was Daniel.

I was sitting in the living room chatting with my sisters when I answered the phone. According to them my face suddenly transformed into such a perplexed expression that they had to ask, "Who is it?"

"The impossible," I joked. As Daniel laughed, I told my sisters "It's Daniel."

"What! No way. We were just talking about him not long ago, what a big coincidence," Lis replied.

I smiled because I already knew that this was not a coincidence. "How did you get this number? How did you find us?" I asked him.

He reported that about a week before, he'd met a mutual friend at the hospital where he was working. After talking about "the Garcia sisters" as they called us, he asked if he had our contact information. The mutual friend said that was funny because a couple of weeks prior he had met another mutual friend from whom he had gotten my mom's phone number — and that that friend had gotten it from another friend. I was delighted listening to this narrative, and I saw clearly how the universal web of life keeps us all connected through the power of synchronicity.

After we talked for a while he asked if it was okay for him to visit, as he had been thinking about me. I was ecstatic. "Me, why have you been thinking about me?"

"I don't know. The memory of you has been popping into my mind," he replied.

"You know, it's amazing that we are talking today since only a month ago I was living in Europe."

I told him he could visit the following weekend. He agreed and we set a date. That evening I felt sick to my stomach because even though I have had many mystical experiences in my life, I felt nervous about seeing him again. This moment reminded me nothing is impossible.

The day he came to visit, my youngest sister, my mom and I were home. We were all excited because we hadn't seen him for such a long time, but I was also anxious because I didn't know what to expect. All the prior week I just kept thinking, *What if I am not into him* — but that was not the case. He had matured, and seemed more intelligent and charming than when he was younger. I didn't know what was happening but I could see only the best in him. We all talked nonstop for hours; after all, there was much catching up to do. We learned about his experiences as a doctor and, most importantly, that he was single. Recently he had broken up with his fiancé whom he had been dating for many years.

I was still talking to Tom. We missed each other deeply, but as the weeks passed the distance between us grew. Daniel kept calling and coming to visit every chance he got, and the closer we became the farther away I felt from Tom. Over time, a very strong attraction grew between Daniel and I. About three weeks after his first call, he took me to lunch at a very nice restaurant. We went for a walk and spent a couple more hours chatting at a coffee shop. On the way home we were caught in a lot of traffic, and while sitting in the car he grabbed my hand and held it tightly. We turned to look at each other, and right there in the middle of the traffic we kissed. That day, every single traffic light from the coffee shop to my house turned red, and every time we had to stop, we kissed, until we were interrupted by the sound of someone's horn. We just laughed and kept driving. That was the first and only time in my life that I ever truly enjoyed being caught in traffic.

Even though Daniel was busy working at the hospital, we would spend every moment of his free time together. By now my relationship with Tom was finally over. Only two months into our relationship, Daniel asked me to marry him. We quickly walked into a courthouse and got married. This was a way for us to feel closer; however, we didn't move in together because we didn't have the means. He was still living with his father so he could save enough money to buy a place someday.

A few months into the relationship, I had a vision while meditating in my mom's living room. I saw the same little girl from my vision in Scotland; again, she was running around and giggling. Three or four years old, she was slim with light brown, curly hair, and her skin glowed. She was wearing a sleeveless, long white dress with little red squares and a thin red ribbon around the bodice. She stopped in front of a pool of bright blue water, and as she was leaning down to touch the water she looked at me, and smiled. Right there I put my hands on my belly and thought, *No way, is Ana here?* Then I opened my eyes, feeling agitated.

Since everything between Daniel and I happened in such a miraculous way, and I found Daniel to be open-minded, I told him about my early vision of Ana while in Scotland. Even though he wanted a family, we had been very careful using birth control as we were not planning to have children any time soon. He had just been accepted into one of the most prestigious hospitals in Colombia to become a specialist in ophthalmology. This meant studying very hard for the next few years, while making little money.

Therefore, when the pregnancy test came back positive, the news felt like a bucket of icewater. Daniel and I were not young kids anymore. We were both in our late twenties, but I was still living in my mom's house with no real job and not a coin in my pocket. Living at home had proven to be a big challenge, and I'd been looking for a job nonstop since I returned to Colombia. After distributing almost fifty resumes I finally got an offer to work as a volunteer for the Colombian Navy, assisting in a review of scientific papers. When I wasn't doing this or looking for a paying job, I dedicated my time to writing my own scientific articles about mangrove ecosystems. All in all, it was a terrible time for a pregnancy.

Daniel's upset was so intense that I began to feel very anxious and disappointed as well. When I was dating Alejandro I had developed tachycardia, which disappeared when I broke up with him, but returned with a vengeance after the pregnancy news. My tachycardia episodes became so severe that I required the use of medication, so besides feeling sad I was also very sick. As I meditated, I asked God and the Beings of Light, "Why did it have to be this way? Why couldn't it be different?"

We talked for days about what to do, and as my health kept deteriorating we decided to end the pregnancy. Then I had one last vision of the baby girl. She was wearing the exact same outfit, once again giggling and running towards the horizon. She stopped in front of the water, turned around and smiled at me. However, this time she was approached by a group of kids that appeared from the horizon. Distracted, she turned away, then turned back, but waved goodbye as she left with the kids.

Daniel and I never talked about the baby again, and I never mentioned my vision of Ana going away. The guilt I felt for ending the pregnancy was so enormous that for the second time in my life I questioned my spirituality. During those days I forgot everything I had ever learned about self-compassion and forgiveness. Feeling absolutely unworthy of the Beings of Light I thought: *I am nothing, I am no one, I deserve nothing.* And from that day on I decided to cut my connection with the Beings of Light for good. I would never dare to meditate or pray again.

CHAPTER 36

The War Zone

NOT LONG after returning to Colombia, I learned of an upcoming conference on Science and Technology where I decided to present my work about mangroves, which was now published. During the conference I was introduced to a Captain who was leading the only two Naval Research Centers in Colombia, and he invited me to another conference at his agency.

The day I walked into the building I stopped in front of a big mural, and experienced a vision of working at this agency. I witnessed an office where two men wearing black Navy uniforms were sitting across from each other at a long table, waiting for me to arrive for an interview. Then the vision ended. I didn't know when or how this was going to happen, so in the meantime I continued looking for a job.

A couple months later, my sister Lis got me an interview with a Navy Admiral through her contacts in the Air Force Reserve. This Admiral was the head of the Maritime Directorate of the Colombian Navy, and he contacted the same Captain I had met a few months earlier. The building where the interview would be conducted was the same one as in my vision.

In fact, the whole scene was exactly as I had seen it. Although the interview was a success they said that there weren't any job openings at the moment, but I would be first on the list. They also asked me if I would help review scientific papers written at the research centers until something else became available. I accepted the offer to work as a volunteer position and waited patiently.

Ten months after the interview, a position as the head of the Marine Biology and Ecology Division became available at the Naval Research Center, located in the jungles of the Pacific Coast of Colombia in a city called Tumaco. Although I was excited for the great opportunity I was also troubled that the research center was in the middle of a war zone. I would have rather gone to the other facility located on the Caribbean Coast. But since this was the only good offer I received after a year and a half of searching, I was not going to let it pass.

During those days Daniel was busier than ever, and I felt lonely and depressed. As a marine biologist, getting back to the coast was the opportunity I needed to continue my career. So, after a long discussion we both agreed that this was my best option. I accepted the job and in January 2000, I packed my bags and left.

Although Colombia had been waging war against revolutionary armed forces and drug cartels for decades, I'd never directly experienced this kind of rage and hatred from other humans while living in the big city. Once in Tumaco, I was exposed to both war and extreme poverty. The research center, together with the Port Authority, was located on a small base on an island called El Morro (The Hill). These facilities were gated and protected by the Marines, which had a base about a mile away, protecting the island connected to Tumaco by a long bridge.

The base where I worked was beautifully kept and comfortable, but the world outside the gates was poverty-stricken. Before I went to Tumaco I learned that the only reason the research facilities were so nicely kept was to motivate the scientists working there to stay on the job. But hardly anyone had stayed longer than three years. I didn't realize how hard it was to live in a war zone until I experienced it myself.

The very first day I arrived, there was a gunfight at 2:00 a.m. right outside the base. Assigned a room at the barracks, my room-mate was the girl I came to relieve. She had been working there for almost three years, so her immediate reaction to the noise was to drop to the floor and yell for me to hide underneath the bed. It was extremely terrifying. I was absolutely sure that I was not afraid of dying, which to me would be the equivalent to heaven. However, I was afraid of what might happen before death; would I be tortured, raped, kidnapped, blinded, seriously injured…?

I began rehearsing in my head what to do under attack. People around there were so used to facing violence and death that the value of life was different from what I was used to, especially since I had always been extremely sensitive to acts of violence.

One day some construction workers were repairing the roof of my laboratory when a hammer fell through the ceiling and hit the ground with a loud bang. I ran out of the lab and yelled, "Watch out what you are doing, you could have killed someone!"

"One more death, what difference does it make?" they replied in an attitude of nonchalance.

I thought they were joking at first, but people were killed close by every day. In most cases the news didn't even bother to report the killings anymore, as it was just daily routine. Only the mass mur-ders made the news, which in itself was extremely shocking.

We were taught how to shoot, which for me was like entering into a forbidden territory. Under Colombian law it is unlawful for civilians to carry any kind of weapon. So, the only time I had touched a gun before was when my dad worked for the Security Service Agency in Colombia. I was around thirteen years old when he took us to the shooting range to shoot his 9mm pistol. He showed us how much damage it could cause and told us that we never should touch it unless we needed it for self-defense. Seventeen years later, when an M4 rifle was handed to me, I was shaking like a leaf.

After passing the tests to hold a gun safely and shoot a target, I felt more confident. With time and practice, I became more accurate. I hoped I never had to take a life, but learning gave me the option of defending myself and other innocents if needed. So, as I experienced war, I understood that guns were just tools that can be good or bad depending on the person who holds it. How could I judge someone that found in a weapon the means to save his life or the lives of others? We also held attack drills because we were under the constant pressure of 'what if'. There is nothing worse than living under the uncertainty of being attacked. When going into the field to collect samples, we always had to bring with us two fully-armed Navy men.

To make matters worse, this area was known for tsunami catastrophes, which meant another kind of drill. After a few months it was clear to me why no one could last in the job for more than three years. Living in survival mode 24/7 could certainly destroy anyone.

Apart from the multiple stress factors of the environment, the work at the Research Center was highly demanding because we were always short on people. I used to work 10 to 15 hours a day, including most weekends and holidays, to keep up with the workload. I never earned any money for the additional hours and the pay wasn't good to start with. The unemployment rate in Colombia was very high and since the country was fighting a war, most government funding was diverted to that purpose. Only four percent of the budget was assigned for science, so I actually felt grateful to have a job.

After a year in Tumaco, the circumstances of the job started to take their toll. Daniel and I were still together but I began to lose interest in everything, including our relationship. He couldn't understand why my nature had changed so much, and I wasn't able to explain it either. I just knew that I felt very negative and depressed. Little by little all the sorrows of my life started to overwhelm me.

Daniel couldn't relate to my feelings, which increasingly affected our relationship. During one of my visits to Bogota to cheer me up, he proposed that we finally have our big, fat wedding with all our family and friends. We could formalize our relationship in front of everyone, since our first wedding was done in secret. After being so low, the idea actually cheered me up, so we agreed and set a date.

I didn't have much vacation time. Once in a while I would go to Bogota during a holiday weekend. Daniel was usually very busy, but he would find a little time for us to be together and plan our wedding. Meanwhile my tachycardia episodes worsened, to the extent that I required an exploratory heart procedure called cardiac mapping, which is done to study the heart's electrical activity. The results were inconclusive and I had to continue taking medicine.

The first year working in Tumaco, I barely left the base until I became very good friends with a local girl named Sandy. She was able to change the course of my life during those days, showing me that it was possible to have fun even in the middle of such hard times. We started to go to the beach during the weekends, exercise together, eat outside the base, and meet new people. As I started to see things differently I was able to relax and feel more energetic. Soon the tachycardia episodes substantially diminished. I started to feel the need to go outside the base more often, to meet people and try new things. I even got over the fear I had for motorcycles and started riding again.

However, Daniel didn't see things the same way, so he would get very mad and jealous if I mentioned anything that he considered outrageous. "You have already done enough crazy things in your life," he would shout. "I will never allow our children to be as crazy as you, jumping up and down like a crazy goat." His comments hurt because he was not accepting the person I was.

We would talk on the phone every night and I had to assure him that I was going straight to bed after we talked. For the first year that was exactly what I did, but when things started to change, I began lying to keep him calm. The last thing I wanted was a war in the middle of a war. So, I would hang up the phone and unplug it in case he would call later to verify my whereabouts. I knew that this wasn't being honest, but I didn't feel like arguing over nothing. I was trying to feel less trapped in my situation, so the more he tried to control me the more I slipped away.

I was never a jealous person. I trusted Daniel with all my heart so I couldn't understand why he couldn't do the same with me. During the first two and a half years of our relationship I proved to him that he could trust me, but once in Tumaco I understood that the problem wasn't just me. He had many insecurities, and had been projecting them over and over on each one of his relationships. As a matter of fact, one of the first things that he ever told me was, "If you ever cheat on me it will be over" and later, "It has been challenging for me to get over that you have lived with someone before." I thought that over time we could work with his insecurities and fix them together. But after being far away from him for more than a year, I started to see things from a different perspective.

I realized that there was nothing I could do to help fix him and began to release the need that I had developed for trying to control and resolve the situation. Soon, it became clear to me that our relationship was over the day I had to start lying to get away with whatever silly thing I was doing. If it was like this now, how would it be after we officially tied the knot? It was then that I decided I didn't want to get married. The decision was extremely hard because in many ways he was an incredible guy. Yet after my relationship with Alejandro, I was sure that I didn't want to deal with another possessive being.

Back then it was extremely hard for me to express my true feelings, especially if it involved hurting someone, so it took a while for me to finally tell Daniel that the marriage was over.

One month before the wedding I went to Bogota intending to tell him the truth, but I just couldn't. He noticed that something was wrong, and instead of trying to understand he got very defensive. He was trying to blame the situation on the fact that I had met new people. I tried to explain that the problem was not other people but his own actions that were pushing me away. But he couldn't see it, so during that visit things only got worse.

Back in Tumaco I was so tormented that I couldn't talk to him, even as the day of the wedding was coming closer. I could barely sleep, eat, or think clearly. The invitations for the wedding had been sent; everything had been booked and organized; the food, the cake, and the flowers had been ordered and every other detail had been carefully managed. Everything was ready including my beautiful wedding dress, made for me by a designer. The last time I put the dress on while still in Bogota I thought, *How sad it is that the most astonishing dress is being worn by the most unhappy girl.*

Only one of my friends knew about my intentions, to which he said, "Think carefully. Daniel is a good guy, and in the end nobody is perfect." I knew all that was true but I couldn't change my mind. Finally decided to call my sister Lis, expecting the worst since Daniel was also her friend, but I was enormously relieved when she said, "If you don't want to marry him then don't do it." After talking to her I called my dad and after explaining the whole situation to him, his answer was the same.

Knowing that two of the most important people in my life supported me, I finally gained the strength I needed to call Daniel and tell him that I couldn't marry him. He said he couldn't live without me, he would never want to meet or marry anyone else, and that he was going to kill himself. Yet none of that happened, and about six months later he met someone else, going on to get married and have a beautiful baby boy.

Some time after our relationship ended, I realized that just as Daniel had to overcome his ghosts, I had to overcome mine as well. The story with Daniel was very similar to the one with Alejandro, in which I experienced a mix of fear, neediness, guilt, anxiety, oppression, and confusion. I saw that I was repeating a pattern which wasn't going to end unless I was able to overcome the fear I had about trusting myself and being on my own. Although I was a loner in many ways, I always had been petrified about the idea of being alone. I had always looked for someone to validate my actions, and help me feel safe and secure.

I needed to regain my power, which I kept giving away every time I turned a partner into a fearful father figure. Thanks to the last relationship, I learned that there was nothing more important than being honest, not just with others, but with ourselves as well. Learning to listen to our heart, to connect and follow our deep emotions, is essential to recognizing our own shadows. Then we can truly embrace the totality of who we are.

During the years I spent in the war zone, I also learned that I didn't have to please everyone, and that it was self-loving to put my needs first. Besides not getting married, I cut my daily working hours to eight, so I could enjoy whatever life could offer. I knew that I had disappointed many people, including my mom. But the more I let go of all the tensions I had built up in the war zone, the lighter and calmer I became. My depression and sadness weren't gone, but at least I was able to see that light could be seen even during the darkest hours.

CHAPTER 37

The Quarantine

A FEW MONTHS after Daniel and I broke up I went on an Oceanographic Cruise to the Eastern Pacific Ocean. My job required that every year I participate in a survey to collect bathymetric, oceanographic, meteorological, and biological data for the Colombian Navy. During this trip I got terribly sick. We were more than 300 miles away from the Colombian coast when I started to get very high fevers that made me shiver uncontrollably. I fainted a few times. There was not an actual medic on board, and the only person capable of giving first aid thought I might have contracted malaria. After all, I was living in the tropical jungles along the Pacific Coast of Colombia where malaria was prevalent.

Since there was no one who really knew, the ship had to make its way back to port. We headed to the port of Buenaventura. Once there, the ship was anchored a few miles away and I was brought to shore on a boat, then taken to a small hospital where they discovered that I had contracted Typhoid fever. I was given very strong antibiotics and sent back to the ship, with instructions to see a doctor on the base in Tumaco.

Once the ship was on its way to Tumaco, I started to feel worse. I became weak, lost my appetite, experienced headaches and delirium. I started to dwell about the Beings of Light and while being in a fever induced delirium state I pleaded, "God/Beings of Light, if this is my time to go please take me, I am ready." This repeated a couple more times and every time I talked to them my condition seemed to improve briefly.

Most of the people onboard didn't realize how sick I was, and in fact I hid it until one day I simply collapsed. At the time, I hated to be the center of attention, and surrounded by men, I didn't want to show any weakness. Only when we arrived in Tumaco five long days later did I surrender; as soon as I saw the doctor, a waterfall of uncontrollable tears burst from my eyes.

When the ship finally arrived in the bay of Tumaco it was instructed to anchor about a mile away from the coast. Typhoid is a life-threatening illness caused by a bacterium called Salmonella Typhi. The infection may be spread through food or drinking beverages contaminated with the bacteria, which is present in sewage waters, flying carrier insects, or people who are shedding the disease. Since it was unknown how I contracted this illness and whether anyone else on the ship was infected, the ship was ordered to remain in quarantine until everyone onboard could be tested.

Because my condition had deteriorated, I was the only one taken away from the ship and brought to the hospital at the Navy base. Several cases of Typhoid fever had been already reported along the Pacific Coast and in some instances the results had been fatal. Due to the severity of the situation the doctor had been instructed to put any patients carrying this disease under isolation. So I was secluded in one wing of the hospital.

Everybody tested negative except the girl I was sharing a bathroom with. Since this disease has an incubation period of up to twenty days before it manifests, everyone was ordered to take antibiotics for a certain amount of time and later they had to be retested. After analyzing the situation, the Navy's doctors concluded that I had to have been contaminated before I boarded the ship. After a few days everybody was re-tested and the ship was finally allowed to dock at the pier.

Although I enjoyed my quiet time, it was one thing to be alone by choice and quite another to be required to do so. Even though the disease doesn't spread by air or touch, the main point was to keep me separated so I wouldn't contaminate anyone else from the use of the bathroom or kitchen utensils. I didn't see anyone other than the medical staff for a few days. These days felt like the longest and saddest of my life. At first only my friend Sandy came to see me, and then gradually others, including some who I didn't even expect. They all admitted not coming earlier because they were fearful of contracting the disease.

Knowing people's feelings became a life-changing experience for me, because it helped me realize that people are usually not afraid of each other's essence, but for what the person carries as a result of being exposed to the realities of the world. It is not who we are but what we have become. Throughout my whole life I had been a loner partly because I had always carried the heavy burden of feeling different from others. This disease of the mind had made me fear getting hurt. So I realized that I had actually put myself in isolation many years before.

Since a young age I had tried to adapt to the environment around me by changing my personality to fit into the world of others. Although I have had periods in my life of complete and authentic openness, they had been short. Then, I would go back to my old patterns of trying to adapt, until I would get tired and retreat for a while to my secluded world, where I felt safe and cared for by the Beings of Light.

I also became aware that no matter where I went or lived, I always had the tendency to encounter certain people who were unkind to me. Some of these people had confessed that they didn't know why they didn't like me. In fact, two of my closest friends admitted that in the beginning they deeply disliked me, until they got to know me. Very few people knew about my hidden spiritual life. All these years I had been projecting my insecurities and anger onto the world around me, and then attracting what I had projected.

The reason I felt different from others was because I perceived them as different from me. I believed in unity, but I had established a profound separation. Although I was becoming aware of my situation, overcoming my life patterns didn't look likely to be easy. Learning to love and accept myself was going to take time.

Who would have thought that I could be grateful for getting Typhoid fever — and for encountering unkind people throughout my life? But they taught me that all I needed was to be me, and to accept others and myself without any judgments as part of the Whole. Only when I started to see through the eyes of other people, truly comprehending that no one differed in essence, could I begin to be healed of the disease of separation I had suffered for so many years.

CHAPTER 38

Ready for a New Path

AFTER I healed from Typhoid fever I was tested in Bogota to ensure I hadn't become a permanent carrier of the disease. I was so grateful to hear that all the results had been negative, and I was free of the bacteria. I could have stayed in Bogota for the length of the long upcoming holiday weekend, celebrating Easter with my loved ones, but since my visit wasn't planned my family and friends already had other arrangements. So, I decided to go back to Tumaco since I didn't feel like spending the time alone in the big city.

It was Easter Sunday of April 2002 and I decided to go on my own to the beach. This was something I usually wouldn't do by myself, but Sandy was gone for the weekend and I was bored at the barracks. While lying on the beach reading a book, I saw walking in the distance a group of good-looking guys wearing black shorts and carrying a cooler. They walked toward me and set their cooler close by. Because of how they looked and carried themselves, it was clear that they were military foreigners.

One of the guys sat right next to me pretending not to look at me; I noticed that on a few occasions he had turned his head just a little to look. I was wearing sunglasses and I never moved the book I was reading away from my face, or turned my head to look at him.

However, I was turning my eyes all the way to the corner to be able to see him. It was clear we both were playing the game of *I-am-not-looking*. After a while, he and his buddies stood up and left.

Although I found him very attractive, I wasn't interested in talking to anyone at the moment. Right after he left I turned over to lie on my belly so I could see which direction he was going. I saw that the group was heading toward a group of Colombian Marines. They were playing volleyball and having fun. He was very handsome so I kept admiring him from the distance.

A while later, just when I decided to go back to the base, the Navy's doctor who had treated me for Typhoid recognized me and yelled. After I greeted the doctor from afar, he shouted, "Come on Ingrid, let me introduce you to my new friends" and he pointed at the group of gringos. I met everyone except the one who sat next to me on the beach. He was sitting on a bench acting cool and indifferent, but as we approached he looked at me, then stood up and said in Spanish, "*Hola como estas, mi nombre es Miguel* (Hi, how are you doing, my name is Michael)."

"Nice to meet you too Michael, my name is Ingrid," I replied. "You can relax because I know English."

The look on his face was one of relief, then he laughed and said, "Thank God! Please call me Mike."

We played volleyball and talked for a while on the beach. When the evening approached he asked me if I wanted to go with the group to eat dinner. I said that I didn't have any extra clothing with me, but he asked the doctor if the driver could take me to the base so I could change and meet them at the restaurant. The doctor didn't disagree and since I didn't have anything else planned, I played along. On the way to the restaurant I thought, *Wow, how convenient that I met the doctor of the base. At least the Typhoid fever keeps leaving positive things behind!*

We had a really good time that evening. During dinner I learned that this had been the very first day since the team's arrival in Tumaco, two months prior, that they had been allowed to leave the base.

They belonged to the US Navy Special Forces and were part of a team specializing in riverine combat. Their sole purpose was to give tactical training to the Colombian Special Forces. These guys were trained to deal with the most stressful situations all over the world, so if I could learn to have fun living in a war zone, they surely could.

During the dinner I joked to Mike, "You are so lucky that the only day they let you free I was right there all by myself at the beach." After dinner he asked if we could meet again to which I nodded in agreement. I didn't know when I was going to meet him again because they had a hectic schedule, and their mobility was very restricted. For security reasons it was forbidden for them to leave the Marine base without permission.

About a week later I was sitting in the cafeteria eating chicken soup for lunch when I turned my head, glimpsing something in my peripheral vision, and saw someone at the end of the corridor wearing a jungle camouflage uniform with his face half painted. He was staring at me. When I saw him he simply smiled and said, "Hey it is me, I am glad to meet you again."

Right at that instant I was shocked to realize that Mike was the man of the vision I had erased from my mind many years ago. I was caught completely off-guard and dropped my spoon. It was as if I had seen a ghost. As I stood up and walked toward him, the clearer the recognition became. His image was the exact same picture that was revealed to me twenty-three years before, at the age of nine. I was so overwhelmed that I told him that I was busy and had to go back to work at the laboratory, even though it was a Saturday. He walked with me to the lab, revealing that with the help of his buddies had done the impossible, coming to visit me this day. I thought: *I believe you, I am sure of that.* At this point I knew that the universe was conspiring to bring us together. Before he left he asked me if I could come in the evening to visit him at his base. "I don't know, I am pretty busy, I will try," I said, stumbling over my words.

I really liked the guy but at this point in my life I wasn't planning to be involved in any serious relationship. It was only a few months since I had ended my own wedding. I also knew that he was going to leave some time soon, so what was the point of getting close anyway? For the rest of the day I dithered about going to see him, then decided, *Why not? I just have to be honest with him and let him know that I am not interested in anything more than a friendship.*

After that evening I went to visit him at his base many other times, always with the understanding that we were only going to be friends. A few times at the beginning he tried to get closer or reach for my hand, but I always made him stop. He could have chosen to meet someone else but we really enjoyed each other's company. So for the next two months that he was in Tumaco we managed to meet as friends almost every day. This was one of the times in my life when I fought the hardest against my own deep desires. However, in the end it paid off, because today I think that by not getting romantically involved we really had the chance to get to know each other on a different level.

On a Saturday afternoon two days before Mike was to leave Tumaco, the Colombian Marine personnel organized a barbeque on the beach to express their gratitude to the US Navy team. I was invited to the party. At the end of the event around 5:00 p.m., drivers from the base packed two trucks with people but had to leave eight of us for the next trip.

I sat on a beach chair while Mike kneeled on the sand right in front of me holding his backpack in front of his body. We were chatting when suddenly everyone became silent, as we all began admiring one of the most beautiful sunsets I had seen since I moved to Tumaco. However, after the sun went down I started to get very worried because it was not safe to be on the beach after dark, especially with a group of North Americans. About 45 minutes later the driver finally showed up and took us all to Mike's base.

Once at the base Mike said to me, "This definitely has been the most romantic evening of my life."

"Why?" I asked. After the sunset, being at the beach at night had been nerve-wracking for me.

"Because this evening while I was sitting on the beach with a beautiful woman I had my hands inside my backpack where I was holding a 9mm pistol in one hand and a concussion grenade in the other. I was planning every move I would have to make to protect you from a threat."

For Mike, this was perfection. I was amazed that he could see something so magical in a situation I would rather not have experienced. After listening to his words and realizing how much he cared about me, I simply couldn't hold back the feelings I had developed for him anymore. That night I kissed him for the first time.

To me he was a strong warrior with an enormous heart willing to protect everyone with equal passion. He was so humble and genuine in his behavior that it was impossible not to be touched by his energy. He had reached deep into my heart.

The night we kissed, we also spent hours talking and looking up at the stars. As the night wore on we found that there weren't any available drivers to bring me back to my base, so Mike found an inflatable mattress and made me a bed. We lay down together and as we were kissing I told him that I wasn't ready to have sex. "We won't do anything that both of us don't agree to do," he said. That evening, Mike made me feel so safe and loved that I just snuggled into his arms. We slept peacefully for the remaining hours of that night.

The next day we were up very early, and I left because he had to spend the morning packing. He asked me to come back after lunch and then we spent the rest of the afternoon together. That evening at the airport we hugged and kissed. Before he had to board the airplane he held my hands tightly and said, "The last thing I ever expected was to meet the woman of my dreams in the middle of a war zone." Then he held my face in his hands while looking at me directly into my eyes and said, "Ingrid, I love you."

"Michael, I love you too," I answered, feeling shaky and sad. If I was supposed to marry Mike, then this could not be the end. And in fact, Mike kept calling and sending e-cards almost every day until the day that we got to meet again. Before we'd met, I had planned a trip to Disneyworld with my dad and my oldest sister. When I met Mike I told him about this trip, but we didn't think that it was a good idea for us to meet during that time because I was going to be with my family. As it turned out, my dad and sister had to cancel, so there was now a great opportunity for us to meet again.

The plan was to visit Miami first, where he would meet me at the airport. Mike had booked a room in a nice hotel on the beach, making sure the room had separate beds since we never had been sexually involved. Once together again, we realized that we were crazy about each other. We spent a few days in Miami and then we went to Orlando to visit the land of Mickey Mouse, where we became like little children. We had the greatest time together, but after two weeks we had to go back to reality: his base in Mississippi and my work in Tumaco were waiting for us.

Working with the Colombian Navy and coming to the war zone was something that had to happen for us to meet; otherwise, I would never have been that close to military personnel. Meeting a Special Forces guy from the USA was something I never contemplated. So it became clear to me that I had to experience the war, not just to open my eyes to that dreadful reality, but also to encounter the man that I had been guided to meet from the time I was a nine year old little girl. We don't know what anything is for, so I have learned that it is best to enjoy every single moment of life as it manifests. The less we resist, the more we enjoy the wonders of life.

CHAPTER 39

Nothing Else to Lose

FOR A WHILE the situation around Tumaco became less dangerous, thanks to a very aggressive military operation targeting the rebel forces. Since this was a secret operation most of us didn't know what was happening. One day the sky was swarming with helicopters; this was the first time in the history of Colombia that all the military forces joined together under the same cause. They called it "The Tsunami Operation" because they entered the zone like a rogue wave taking down every rebel in their path.

I was at the airport with my friend Sandy, waiting for a friend of hers to arrive, when suddenly there were airplanes, helicopters, and military personnel everywhere. It felt like we had been transported into a Hollywood movie about the Vietnam War. All the commercial flights had been canceled so we returned to the base to wait for news. Since this happened during a weekend, it felt like forever before we knew something.

Later on, we learned that there was nothing to fear anymore because Tumaco had been the end point of this operation. All the rebels were taken by surprise, and many of them hid their guns, showing themselves as farmers. I don't know how many of these people's lives were spared; according to military personnel the operation was a huge success. One could only hope for the shedding of blood to stop and this senseless war to end. I wondered how much longer Colombians were going to keep killing their fellow Colombians.

But a few months later, the situation in Tumaco worsened. Paramilitary groups were moving into the city, fighting with the rebels and amongst themselves. Most of these groups were funded by money coming from illegal drug trafficking. Each group wanted to claim the lands used for growing illegal plants, and control the farmers and clandestine processing laboratories. Hence the war grew even bloodier than before.

Meanwhile the rebels were blowing up all the communication towers they could reach. They were also stopping all the trucks that carried goods into our region, leaving Tumaco isolated and in need of all kinds of supplies. Things had become scarier than ever before. To make matters worse, we received pamphlets informing us that as civilians working for the government, we were considered military targets. We were advised to be extremely cautious when leaving the base and to not be out late at night. Before, the war never crossed the gates of our base, but recently a couple of petty officers who worked with us had been killed because they got involved with the wrong people.

I talked to Mike whenever I could. "Please leave this place before you end up getting hurt," he urged me. "I am sure that you'll find more opportunities somewhere else." But it took me a while to listen, as I didn't want to become unemployed again. I felt that I needed more time to decide what I was going to do next, even though my deepest feelings urged me to pack my things and leave immediately.

One Saturday around lunchtime I was at the cafeteria eating lunch and talking with a guy who worked with us. While chatting some other men joined the conversation and he said to us, "I'm not going to spend the evening trapped at this base. I'm going out tonight."

"Just be careful," we replied.

He didn't make it. Around 7:00 p.m. he was driving his motorcycle when he was shot to death. This killing shocked everyone because it made us realize that we were indeed being targeted.

I was extremely disturbed about this news, and if that wasn't enough, more bad news was on the way.

After two and a half years of living in Tumaco, the director of the research center and his girlfriend had to leave. He received orders to transfer to the headquarters in Bogota before completing his term. This news felt like a bucket of cold water because they had been some of my closest friends since I moved there. I was upset and worried not just by their departure, but because their successor would be a Captain regarded by all of us as very harsh and controlling. He had some very good ideas, but he wanted to micromanage to the point that his command would feel like a dictatorship.

This kind of behavior didn't suit an environment where most of the workers were civilians dealing not only with normal job pressures, but also the daily stresses of living in a war zone. Most everyone felt that this Captain didn't value the work we were doing, even though most of us were dedicating our lives to this place. When he fired two contractors who had been working in the research center for years, the general resentment escalated and a few scientists wanted to leave.

I'd just about had enough when I got into a heated argument with the new Commanding Officer. He wanted us to go on an oceanographic survey with an instrument that was not insured. Since very little money went to research the loss or damage of any instrument in Colombia, was a very serious matter. I wrote a letter stating that I wasn't going to be responsible for any loss or damage; I showed the letter to my co-workers and all of them co-signed it. When the director got the letter he was furious. However, there was not much time for arguing since I was leaving to work on board the oceanographic survey. So, during the time I was gone, with no means of defending myself, he declared that my intentions were malicious and that I was organizing a coup.

In a way, he was right to be angry because I didn't manage the situation well. Perhaps I should have urged people to write their own letters, but I knew that everyone was too afraid to do so. They deeply feared his reprisal because they couldn't afford to lose their jobs. Nevertheless, my biggest mistake was to act from fear. I'd encountered his aggression before, and seen how he had humiliated some of my co-workers, leading me to regard him fearfully.

During my absence, he ordered my name to be removed from my office and the door of my dormitory. He also ordered the engineering technician to wipe out all of my personal files from the computer and to change the password so I couldn't access information anymore. I knew none of this until I returned to find that I had been literally removed from the system. Infuriated, that very day I wrote my letter of resignation. A few days later, I was out of Tumaco forever.

During the time I worked for the center every person leaving was honored with a going-away party and a plaque, but for me there was nothing. I cried so hard because I had spent three years of my life deeply dedicated to working at this place, despite the fact that almost every day I wanted to be somewhere else. For three years I went to bed every night not knowing if I was going to be alive the next day. But no matter how important it was for me to have a job as a scientist, nothing makes sense when one's life is hanging in the balance and happiness has been completely compromised.

Later on, after recalling all it took for me to leave Tumaco, I laughed when I remembered what the Beings of Light once said: "Sometimes extreme measures are required for us to wake up and realize that it is time to let go and move on."

Until this point in this life I never knew what it really meant to hate anyone, until this Captain crossed my path. For a while I felt intense feelings of anger toward this Captain, whom I considered utterly insensitive. These feelings began to fade away as I recognized that he had been on my path as a lesson for me: learning to let go of not just a job, but also fear and anger.

Such extreme experiences kept bringing me face to face with my most hidden shadows and were leading me to the understanding that my perception about the world was the result of my own projections. At the time I was fighting my own personal war; I was angry at my boss, angry at the war, angry at poverty, and angry that I had to be doing this job because I felt there were no options. Above all I was angry at myself, for feeling disempowered, for not always speaking up, and spending almost all my life being afraid.

CHAPTER 40

Victories and Demons

TWO MONTHS after leaving Tumaco I went back to the USA to visit Mike for the second time, at the end of December 2002. We decided to meet in Miami again and then go to Universal Studios in Orlando. When I first met Mike I told him that I didn't plan to marry. At the end of our day in the amusement park, he asked, "What if I hypothetically asked you to marry me?" We were sitting in the car and he was holding my hand while his big blue eyes were wide open, staring at my face to see my reaction.

"What if hypothetically I would say yes!" I answered.

"Yes, she said yes!" he shouted, but then stopped and asked, "So, is that a true yes?"

"Yes, it is a yes," I laughed.

I'd expected to stay for only two months in the USA, but would never leave. At this point we barely had any possessions or money. Mike lived in a rented, dilapidated trailer in Bay Saint Louis, Mississippi, and his truck was ancient. But compared to me, Mike had a lot. The most expensive possessions I had in Tumaco were a small refrigerator and a 20-inch TV, which I sold when I left. When I came to the USA I was carrying one bag and one thousand US dollars in cash. On the way back from Florida to Mississippi, the truck broke down and the repair cost exactly the money I had in hand.

After the truck was fixed once back on the road, the atmosphere was very quiet until Mike said that he was feeling down about me having to spend all my money on the truck's repair. "Why are you with me, if I don't have anything to offer you?" he asked.

At the time, my attitude was to accept with an open mind everything that came my way. After many years of suffering I was ready to move on. I replied, "Because you and I don't have anything to lose, but I know that together we have everything to gain. We are all that we need."

"But I am poor," he admitted.

"Poor compared to whom? We may not have cash at the moment, but we have everything else we need."

While working with the Colombian Navy in the jungles of the Pacific Coast, I learned to see the difference between people who were happy living in extremely modest conditions, and those who felt miserable. The fundamental difference was that some didn't regard themselves as being poor; according to them nature was giving them all they needed to have a plentiful life. These people had very little or no exposure to civilization.

During one of my oceanographic cruises based in Tumaco, we had the magnificent opportunity to visit a fishing village in the middle of nowhere. The youngest kids of the village had never seen Caucasian outsiders before. We arrived on a small boat launched from the mother ship, and landed on the beach where the little kids were amazed to see our presence. I remember with such delight how they wanted to touch my hair and hold my hand. We offered them chocolate bars and some other small goodies that they regarded as precious jewels. That day I understood clearly that happiness didn't have anything to do with the stuff we accumulate, but with the freedom derived from not needing any materialistic wealth.

I knew that money was the last thing I needed to worry about, because the potential to make money was already there for us. The important thing was for Mike to see that poverty was just a concept that was limiting his mind. He'd always thought that he was an unlucky person, a feeling he acquired when very young. He had a negative outlook stuck deeply in his mind, but after we got together things started to shift. Opportunities arrived, people around us helped, and the money situation simply started to resolve. The more positive we both became, the more things we got. Sometimes he would look at me with puzzled eyes while saying, "Man, none of this ever happened to me before I met you." Mike said he loved the fact that I was the very first person in his life who talked in terms of "we" and not just "me."

We planned and executed a very unconventional wedding, marrying in April 2003 at the NASA base where his Navy Unit was located. He wore his Special Forces Jungle Camouflage uniform while I wore a beautiful, camouflaged black-and-white wedding dress. On our wedding day one of the Special Operations Craft Riverine boats picked up his father and me at a pier on the Jordan River, and brought us to the pier located at his unit. The Justice of the Peace, Mike, and the rest of his team were waiting for us at the pier. By then the war in Iraq had just started, and the people from his unit videotaped the wedding and sent it to Iraq for the guys to have something different to enjoy.

Mike's unit was located at a NASA base named Stennis Space Center. A few months before the wedding, Mike took me on a tour around the base. As he headed down the road in the exact direction I had seen in my vision twenty years before, I felt ecstatic when I recognized the NASA building. I yelled, "Oh shit, I am going to work here!"

"Okay, if that's what you want, we could explore a way for you to work here," Mike said, looking startled.

Turning my head to the other side of the road where I saw a building with a glass frontage, I exclaimed, "I am going to work there as well!"

I asked Mike to drive around the area again, as I was in complete awe. I knew for sure that future employment was there for me. A couple months later, Mike helped me find a job working as a contractor for an environmental agency that was on the base. I was making about $45 an hour, a fortune compared to what I had earned before in my life. One month on this salary was the equivalent to one year at my last job in Colombia. This money allowed us to pay off debts and move to a nice apartment complex.

Eight months later, I learned about an opening position as a technician at the Gulf Coast Research Laboratory at the University of Southern Mississippi (USM). After submitting a resume I was contacted by a professor for an interview, which I went to with the scientific books, articles, and technical reports I had written since graduating from college.

At the beginning of the interview there was only one professor interviewing me, Dr. Rakocinski, but he called in others until I was surrounded by a group of very intelligent and experienced college professors. I was staggered to realize that they were part of the same vision I had when I was twelve. As I was looking at them in amazement, they suggested that I should pursue a graduate program in Coastal Sciences at their facility, and apply for a scholarship, rather than pursuing the technician's position.

After I left the office and got into my car, I was shaking and crying tears of joy because this was beyond anything I had anticipated.

After coming from Tumaco where I felt that my work hadn't been appreciated, I was convinced that what I had done there didn't have much value — despite having written and published several important science articles, and my third book, the last one about oceanography. That day I began to realize that I was wrong. The uncounted hours of time and dedication to the work I did in Tumaco were contributing to my career in a way that I would have never imagined.

Not long after, Dr. Rakocinski told me to present my work at his campus, where I received a lot of positive feedback. Then later, I also presented at the Mississippi Academy of Science, where I got very good reviews. Some of the students there belonged to the Department of Marine Science at USM as well, and after talking to them they told me that I should come visit their campus. Two weeks later I received an official invitation to visit their department, located at the NASA base from my vision. There, I was interviewed by a professor called Dr. Redalge, who was so impressed with my work that he asked me to join the department as a graduate student under his guidance.

Only a few months after the first interview, I was offered a full scholarship to a Masters-PhD program. I was very grateful to Dr. Rakocinski for all his support, but eventually decided I was better suited to the Department of Marine Science located at NASA's Stennis Space Center. So in the fall of 2005, I joined the department to pursue a higher degree in Marine Science with an emphasis in Biological Oceanography. After a few months into the program I met people from other agencies also located at the base, so I presented my research work based on climate variability at the National Oceanographic and Atmospheric Administration (NOAA), the Naval Research Laboratory (NRL), and NASA's

Applied Science Program of the Earth Science Directorate.

While presenting my work at NASA, I met a very smart scientist, Dr. Castillo, who was impressed with my resume and my work. I told him that I had seen an email in which NASA was offering a grant to support graduate students working with remote sensing satellite imagery and marine optics. Although I already had a full scholarship, I wanted the grant from NASA so my advisor could give the money he was giving to me to another student. I was at first refused because I wasn't a US citizen, but when I called Dr. Castillo to deliver the bad news, he said, "Give me a minute, I will call you later."

After an hour, he called me back to say I'd be granted a fellowship that was already established between NASA and my department.

So that was how the vision I had of working with NASA — when I was just that twelve-year-old little girl walking down the street with my mom and wondering about the unknown future — became real when I was thirty-four. Who could I have ever known when I was twelve that some day I could study the oceans using equipment NASA had launched into space? I didn't, but the Beings of Light certainly did.

Although everything about my career and finances were going very well, life at home was a challenge. Being married to a Special Forces soldier had proved to be very difficult. Mike was gone most of the time, and after arriving in the US from a war zone, I carried with me many ghosts. Living alone in a country where I didn't have any friends or family was difficult, and I was still having health issues with my heart. I barely ate, dropped to eighty pounds, and felt very depressed every time Mike left.

To make things even harder Mike's teenage children from his

previous marriage, Kevin and Jessica, came to live with us and I had to raise them mostly by myself. Those days I felt so overwhelmed with school, work, and home responsibilities that I ended up seeing a psychiatrist. I was diagnosed with post-traumatic stress disorder (PTSD) and depression, for which I started to take medication.

In 2006 Mike retired from the Navy and was finally able to be with us at home. I was happy that he was with us, even more so when I learned that I was pregnant. But Mike reacted with deep fear when he learned the news, situation that I perceived as him feeling disappointed; eventually he confessed that at the beginning he got pretty scared because he had just retired. Although he was about to start a new job, he felt a lot of uncertainty about the future.

My negative perception about his reaction brought a lot of sadness into my heart, which was an adverse contributing factor to my troubled pregnancy. The picture I had of a happy husband cheering the news of a new baby was shattered, and deep inside the terrifying feelings of loneliness and rejection I had always carried within arose to the surface. In a similar way as with Ana, I became extremely sick during the pregnancy, unable to eat or drink anything unless I was taking medication. Eventually I had to take leave from the university and NASA.

Despite everything I absolutely adored this baby because I knew that he was the baby boy I had envisioned since I was fourteen. A year before getting pregnant he'd started to appear again. Just like when I was fourteen, he would hide behind doors and furniture waiting for me to find him and then giggle giving himself away. So no matter how sick I was feeling, I was going to have him.

My husband stayed with us only one more month. Then, due to his new job as a private consultant working security in conflicted zones around the world, he had to spend most of my pregnancy away. My stepson helped a little, but there was not much that he could do to help me feel better and my obstetrician didn't have time on his busy schedule to see me. It was then I decided to go to Colombia where I could be around my family and receive some love and help. I expected to spend three weeks there but I was so ill that instead I had to stay for two months. After that, I was feeling strong enough to go back to the USA.

My younger sister Lili agreed to come with me and help until the baby was born. With her help and the assistance of a new obstetrician, the last month of my pregnancy went smoothly. In April 2007, my son David was born one month prematurely, a healthy boy, but weighing only five pounds. By this time my husband, my mom and my youngest sister Fabi had all gathered at our home for the arrival of the baby. Over time I understood how the power of love could cure anything.

When David was one month old, everyone including my step-children and my husband had left, and I was back in charge of everything, on my own. I felt petrified about Mike leaving us, and having to raise David all alone. Only two days after Mike's departure I had to go through the excruciating pain of a kidney stone, but I discovered, once again, that I wasn't alone and that I had amazing strength. During those days my closest neighbors showed their love for me, and I recognized that I had the power to endure and overcome anything.

One month later I went back to work at NASA, finished my post-graduate classes and started to work on my dissertation, while raising the baby pretty much on my own. In May 2009, after a great deal of work, I graduated in record time from my Masters-Ph.D program with a GPA of 4.0. Since I graduated the professors had used me as a role model to show the rest of the students that if

I was able to do it they could do it too.

All those years of pain and suffering turned out to be crucial because they proved that there was nothing I couldn't do. By the way, as David started to grow he looked exactly as I had seen him in my visions. Even now, after ten years, playing hide-and-seek with me still is his favorite game.

CHAPTER 41

Meeting the Dalai Lama

O NCE I finished college, my fellowship with NASA also
ended and new job opportunities arose. I was hired to
work with a US Navy Oceanographic Command, located
in the glass building that I recognized as the other place where I
would work someday. While employed with this agency I had the
chance to do something else I truly love: travelling. Part of my job
requirement as an oceanographer was to participate in surveys
worldwide.

In May 2010 I was sent on a trip to Singapore, and right before
leaving my friend Santiago called me. I mentioned to him that after
completing my assigned work I was planning to take a few days off
and travel around Asia. I didn't know where I was going, so he told
me that he had a very good friend, Rocio, who lived in Malaysia,
and that she could guide me.

She was a Colombian lady who had been living in Asia for
about twenty years. I contacted her through email asking for her
guidance, and received a prompt answer with good advice and an
invitation to Kuala Lumpur. Once there, I felt a very strong connection. We spent hours conversing about spirituality. She was raised
as a Catholic and followed the traditions of her religion diligently,
but lately she had been learning about other philosophical paths.

I spent only three days at her house, but it was as if I had known her and her family forever.

The day before I left to continue my journey to other countries in Asia, she told me, "I am planning to meet the Dalai Lama in Dharamsala (India) in September, and I was wondering if you would like to go?" I was in complete awe because I had wanted to meet the Dalai Lama since I first learned about him through the Beings of Light and my grandma at eight years old.

"Yes!" was my immediate answer.

However, after this joyous moment I remembered that I had a survey trip to the Middle East scheduled for September. At the same time I had the strong feeling that this trip to India was going to happen, so I decided not to worry and leave it in God's hands.

After leaving Malaysia, I went to Cambodia and Indonesia, where I visited a few cities and many different temples. All these wonderful places brought me back to the feelings of joy and happiness that I thought I had lost. It seemed as if I was rediscovering a world I had known before. Everywhere I went I met incredibly nice and open people who wanted to help me, to show me the best of their country and their culture, which made my experiences richer and more satisfying. This was something I truly needed because my heart had been filled with sadness for the past few years. Those days the only thing that kept me going was my little David.

Back in Mississippi I learned that the trip to the Middle East had been re-scheduled from September to the beginning of October. After learning the incredible news I felt grateful to the Beings of Light.

The trip to India was going to take almost three weeks. Rocio, a couple of her friends, and I were going to spend one week in

Dharamsala receiving the Dalai Lama's teachings; the rest of the time we would spend traveling around a few other cities in India. So, my next big task was to tell my husband, who was coming back from Iraq, that I wanted to go to India to meet the Dalai Lama. My trip to the Middle East would last for two and a half months, so telling him that I wanted to leave three weeks earlier was not easy.

However, after telling him how important this trip was to me, I received his support. He knew that he had been gone from home a lot and that for the past seven years I had been working nonstop and taking care of everything at home. "I guess you deserve a little time off," he said. The more everything worked out my way, the more I knew that this trip was meant to be.

Although many great things had happened to me since I moved to Mississippi, the path had not been easy. During those days it seemed like the pursuit of happiness in our family was almost impossible. Every time my husband was absent he said that he felt unhappy because he was gone. But at home he felt unhappy as well, because he didn't have anything that he enjoyed doing there.

I tried to support him in any way I could. He had his dream job and I didn't want to become an obstacle in his path. After a few years, when David was around three, I felt that I'd had enough. I felt that David and I were only a burden to Mike; consequently, I was tired, unhappy, and extremely angry. The sensation was like an arrow piercing all the way through my chest; night or day, I couldn't get rid of this intensely painful feeling.

I thought that meeting the Dalai Lama would change my mental and emotional condition, so I invested all my faith on this trip. The night before I met him I felt extremely excited, and was grateful and filled with emotion after receiving his teachings. But as the days passed I realized that things were not going to work the way I had expected. I was thinking that I could find in the outer world what I believed I was lacking, without looking toward my inner world. Nevertheless, this was the beginning of a deep transformation that I couldn't foresee.

The day before the teachings ended we had the opportunity to meet the Holiness' healer. She had an astonishing bright aura and I could see how light emanated from her eyes. She was one of the most powerful yet delicate and humble women I have ever met. In her presence I sensed the same healing energy that flows from a beautiful flower. "Could you help me to heal my troubled heart?" I asked her.

"Your problem is not in your heart, but in your mind," she answered. As she started to perform a ritual for me, she added, "Your mind is so filled with thoughts that there is no room for you to become still and tranquil. Because of that, your whole self is out of balance."

On the way to meet the healer, I'd had a very sad vision. One of the ladies that I had met on the trip had been married to her husband for more than twenty-five years. She thought they were happy together and would be married forever. But that day I saw that their relationship was going to end soon. I didn't say anything to them, but while at the healer's workplace I realized she was right: I wasn't keeping my head in the present, but was preoccupied with many thoughts, including my past life experiences and visions of the future. I wasn't meditating anymore, so I realized that the only way to return to alignment was to start quieting my busy mind.

That night after visiting the healer we all went together to eat dinner at a restaurant. I was pretty quiet, mostly listening and thinking about the healer's words. Then I started to feel a tingling sensation in the palm of my hands, which were resting on my lap.

When I looked down I saw very delicate sparkles of energy coming from my hands. I excused myself and ran to the bathroom to examine my hands, and saw that my palmistry lines were showing two perfectly star-like shapes, one on each hand. For the first time in a long while I felt the strong presence of the Beings of Light.

I said nothing about this at dinner, but back at the hotel I felt more comfortable to talk to my roommate, Begoña. When she saw my hands, she exclaimed, "Oh my God! Those are definitely stars and they are glowing! I would have never believed something like this if I hadn't seen it with my own eyes." She wanted to call everyone's room but it was really late and I felt shy about it.

The next day she asked me if she could talk to the others about the stars. I agreed and during breakfast time I showed them my hands. The stars were not glowing anymore but they were still clearly visible. Everyone was making comments about what the stars could mean when a Chinese lady approached me, politely asked if she could look at my palms and said, "You are going to travel to many places carrying a spiritual message." I looked at her with a smile and bashfully said, "Thank you." She smiled back and left. At that very moment I remembered when the Beings of Light told me that someday I was going to pass their teachings onto many others.

The last day of the teachings in Dharamsala, I joined the Dalai Lama's Refuge Ceremony, which signifies the beginning of a spiritual path. According to the Buddhist teachings, this path enables followers to transform limitations, negative patterns, and confusion. "Taking refuge" thus means liberation from the suffering that human beings habitually experience.

After the ceremony we were allowed to have some pictures taken with the Dalai Lama. I was delighted and deeply grateful when I was able to sit next to him and hold his hand, as he emanated pure love and peacefulness. Unfortunately, since my mind was still so busy I couldn't deeply share the stillness of this joyous moment. I was actively looking into the library of my mind to find something to say to him. It was as if my ego needed to reassure it-self, when in the end all I had to do was surrender and simply be present.

Thankfully, I didn't find anything to say — and that day I decided that I was going to find a way to get back to the root of my awareness. I recognized that the bitterness, anger, and sadness I had developed over the years were the result of having lost my connection with my Inner Self. I had to reconnect with the Source and allow myself to vibrate as the being of light I knew I was. Sadly, I was so trapped in the illusion of being a victim, asking "Why me?" that I would descend to lower levels of depression before I would be able the see the Light once again.

CHAPTER 42

Two Magical Words

A FTER MY trip to India I was supposed to spend two and a half months in the Middle East. However, my travel from the city of Agra to the New Delhi airport was interrupted by a serious car accident, and I had to be medically evacuated back to the USA. Despite having a head and neck injury, I was grateful because I was promptly reunited with my little David. I had been praying for the days to pass quickly so I could be back to him. So I realized once again that even in those experiences we may interpret as negative there is something to be thankful for.

Only a couple of weeks after returning home I learned that the couple whom I had met in India, after being married for more than twenty-five years, did split up. These unexpected changes reminded me of the Beings of Light saying, "Nothing is permanent for anyone in the world of the form." I had been living a stagnant life, feeling helpless and angry; now more than ever I wanted a change. The more I allowed the world around me to dictate my emotional state, the angrier and more depressed I became.

When I arrived home from India, Mike jokingly said, "It is easier to be in Iraq fighting the war than taking care of a three-year-old." But in my state of mind plus combined with the fact that Mike hadn't celebrated my pregnancy with David only made me more frustrated. I didn't say much to him at the time because I wanted things to go smoothly; I was trying to make the brief moments he had at home happy and harmonious. Yet, in the middle of this apparent peace, a bigger battle was developing in my heart.

A second after he left and I was on my own, feeling alone and helpless, my whole world crumbled. I felt that emotionally I was nothing but a failure. None of my relationships in the past had worked and I perceived that this one was failing also, even though we loved each other deeply. My dream of David having a close relationship with his father also appeared unreachable since Mike was going to continue to be gone between six and nine months every year. It was so sad to think that the need of money had turned into the main objective of our lives. It hit me hard when one day after Mike left David asked me, "When is Daddy going to visit us again?" Then I realized that Mike was indeed but a visitor. *Why did I make the choice of marrying this one?* I wondered, feeling profound sorrow.

We had moved to a new city where I didn't know anyone and I didn't have any close friends despite living for seven years in the USA. I realized that I had been so busy that I never made the time to engage in any friendships. Besides all my daily responsibilities the health of David and I had been fragile so I had to spend many hours going to doctors and hospitals hindering the possibility of having any time for rest or having fun.

On the other hand, although my new job allowed me to travel, I hated to be away from David and Mike, so this one didn't seem to be the right job either. I felt that I despised the way everything in my life was going. To make things worse after going to India I recognized how disconnected I had become from the only thing that had given me true joy in my life, the Beings of Light. I missed them so much but the guilt I carried about the mistakes I had made in my life kept me away from them. I felt so deeply regretful and melancholic that I started to fall into the deepest depression I had ever experienced, to the point that I felt paralyzed. It was hard to drag myself out of bed and move.

The memories of my near-death experience became so vivid that I wanted to go back to that place of bliss. I didn't want to be part of this world anymore. I didn't want to continue living one more day. Though I wanted a change I couldn't find my way out. The only reason to keep on going was David, as I would never leave my baby alone. Consequently, when a tiny insane idea that maybe David and I could leave this world together crossed my mind, I decided that I needed serious help, and prayed to the Beings of Light like never before.

The very next day I found a psychologist through a friend's recommendation. I started by telling the psychologist the usual stories regarding the many reasons why I was angry then later I moved to all the different sufferings that I have had throughout this life. Following a few months of consultation, one day he suggested that I make a list of my biggest sufferings. The list was so long that it was overwhelming. After looking at the list he looked at me and said, "In my thirty-five years of practice I have never met anyone who has suffered this much and is still mentally stable."

I didn't know how to reply at first, then asked, "Why did all of these things have to happen to me? Why me?"

"Why not?" he answered matter-of-factly.

Those two words changed everything; they were the missing link that I needed to hear. Then he added, "Thanks to all that, you have become the unique person that you are. Look what you have accomplished, the places that you have visited, the people that you have met and all the incredible things that you have learned."

That day my perception had shifted and I was able to recognize myself as the cause of everything, rather than an effect. For the very first time I didn't perceive myself as a victim. I also realized that none of the past was here anymore, and what remained was a profound sense of *Self* that was unchangeable and magnificent.

A few days later, as I was still immersed in this astonishing and liberating state of mind, my depression finally ended and has never come back. I was in the process of reorganizing my walk-in closet, thinking about all the party clothes I had not been able to wear since I married, when I realized that I was stuck in yet another chapter of my troubled life. Standing in the middle of this small closet I realized how insignificant the story of "me" was, meanwhile sensing a vast universe alive within me. I realized that there was so much that I couldn't see, sense, or learn because I had been trapped in the narrative of "poor me." I immediately moved to the window and opened the blinds, flooding the room with light.

Suddenly I could perceive value in all the events that had ever happened in my life, and a profound sense of appreciation arose within me. Since I was very young I always envisioned myself as a bird — because besides the feeling of freedom that birds evoke, they can see the whole picture from above. Now I could finally become the bird of my vision. Not only could I value all my experiences, I could appreciate that the most difficult challenges had brought me to ask important questions about my existence. These key questions inevitably led me to remember that I already had all the answers within me. Today, I know that I was meant to experience life the way I did so these answers could be comprehended.

From the time I was a little girl I always felt as if I was an observer. In young adulthood I was able to ask, "What is that that I am observing?"

"All of life," the Beings of Light answered, then after a pause they added, "through your personal experience."

This helped me understand the unique importance of my existence. I know that although we are one with the Whole, each of us is a unique emanation of the One, or God, or Whole. This is why the Beings of Light always referred to each one of us as special. Nothing in the universe lacks purpose. Every one of us is special because of the unique way in which we experience and perceive life. We are part of the universal flow of infinite creation always reinventing itself, manifesting, and eternally expanding.

After my depression ended, I kept visiting the doctor for a while longer because I enjoyed talking to him. However, my conversations with him started to change dramatically. I was seeing value where I never saw it before, and I wanted to keep sharing my excitement with him — especially since everything was happening at such a fast pace. Only a few months before I'd wanted to die, and now I was tasting total bliss.

Not long after, I informed the doctor that I didn't need to come back anymore. He said that he had been waiting for this day to happen. At that point I had become so fulfilled with everything that I knew I could continue my path without the need of a psychologist, but I told him that he had my friendship forever.

After this awakening, incredible people, beautiful books, and many more amazing experiences regularly appeared on my path. It was like the light of a candle had been lit, and that sole flame had brought clarity to my blinded mind. With every new discovery a deep state of gratefulness began to develop within me. Today, I understand what Eckhart Tolle meant in *A New Earth*: "Suffering has a noble purpose: the evolution of the consciousness and the burning up of the ego. The fire of suffering becomes the light of

Tarot

Rumi's guesthouse

consciousness. The truth is that you need to say yes to suffering before you can transcend it."

As I was experiencing my new state of joy and gratitude, another powerful revelation, similar to the one I experienced on the bus twenty years earlier, arrived near the end of 2010, not long after I turned forty. I was driving and contemplating a beautiful day when out of the blue I started to feel that God, or Source, or Spirit was everything and everywhere. There was nothing that wasn't Source energy. I could breathe it and sense it in every part of my being. Everything that I am was in bliss.

In that moment, the real meaning of Love became utterly clear; *that it is absolutely everything.* That's why, as an infant I could admire my hands with such captivation, or as a toddler admire a piece of lint, and why later I was fascinated to see a cell under the microscope and stars in the vast firmament. It's why I could feel intense closeness with animals, plants and nature, and inexplicable affection for humanity, including deep compassion for everyone who suffers.

Nowadays I can sense love everywhere, even while I am drinking a glass of water every morning. I sense that I am drinking pure energy and bathing all my being with it. It is so pleasing and refreshing, a magnificent way to start the day filled with gratitude. I have also realized that love is not about "being in love" with someone, it is about *being in love with life.* From there you will be able to truly love anyone, starting with yourself. At this point receiving and giving becomes one. Today, I am able to adapt more easily to any circumstances because I am able to appreciate from the heart whatever is being offered to me, and whatever I can give to others. Source adores us, and never stops giving and receiving no matter what.

That day I received the answers to the questions I had asked the Beings of Light twenty years earlier, when I had my first introduction to this feeling while sitting on the bus. It was as if no time had passed since I asked, *Why and exactly when did we stop knowing that we are one with the Whole? How is it even possible to forget what we really are?*

Suddenly, after not hearing the Beings of Light for more than a decade I heard, "One never stopped being *One*; one has never left the *Source*; one just became distracted and seemingly forgot."

After all these years I have learned how easy it is to become distracted and completely merged into the world of the form, filled with expectations, judgments and sufferings. How easy it is to get lost and to perceive life as a roller coaster full of extreme highs, lows, and sharp turns. After I stopped being a victim, everything became more linear in the sense that I discovered nothing had ever been good or bad. I just had been walking the path of experience that led toward waking up. This doesn't mean that since then I haven't encountered challenges and difficulties. But it has become easier to get realigned and find solutions, instead of getting lost in the world of drama and complaints.

Twenty years earlier I had also asked, "Why me?" But this question simply vanished into the understanding that I am the essence of everything, so it is simply impossible to feel unworthy. That day I understood that I was everything that *is*. Everything I had perceived as a separate entity was nothing more than an extension of the Source. I compare this to the exoskeleton of a lobster, where the shell is an extension of the lobster itself — but the exoskeleton is eventually replaced while the lobster remains intact. Only the outer reality, which is the result of our own co-creation, is impermanent, but the essence of creation is eternal.

Through all these experiences I finally understood with deep clarity what the Beings of Light had been trying to tell me: that nothing was as real as it appeared to be, and that the more I would stop identifying with the world of the form, the freer I would become. It matters not how the world moves; what matters is how one perceives it. So much had to happen in my life for me to realize that perception was the key to either maintaining or eradicating all sufferings.

Today I realize that every being including the Beings of Light, the Ascended Masters, the greatest spiritual leaders, and the True Self are all one. We are all part of the same universal consciousness leading us through experience to wake up. I don't know where I am on my journey; I don't really need to know. While in deep meditation I don't look for anything, ask for anything, or expect anything; I simply *Am*. All the while I experience a deep sense of bliss in *being*. I don't know what else is needed; I just know that a profound feeling of wanting to share this divine feeling with everyone else has awakened within me. That's how this book started to happen.

One afternoon while at the beach playing in the ocean waves in Costa Rica, I was caught by a big wave right at the break point. The wave rolled and threw me violently to the sandy floor. When I recovered and went to the surface to catch my breath I was trapped by another wave, then another, until my husband grabbed my arm and pulled me out of the surf. Once out of danger, with my feet still in the water, I realized that I had not felt any fear whatsoever. I looked at the horizon with complete trust, feeling ready for whatever was to come. That day with true intention I said to God, "I am ready to serve." But later that night I found myself pondering the question, "Who am I serving and what can I do for others?"

By way of an answer, the Beings of Light woke me up in the middle of the night with the picture of a purple flower blooming in the air. The heart of the flower contained the essence of me, and surrounding the flower there were hundreds of pictures showing every being, including the people, plants and animals, I had ever tried to help in any possible way or treated with kindness throughout this life, starting from childhood. All the members of my family were on the pictures, my friends and even people I had only briefly encountered. Then I understood that my work had already started many years ago and that I had always been a servant of God.

Epilogue

WITH THE revelations that brought me to understand that I was not a victim and instead the co-creator of my existence, the clearer my life experience became and the more appreciative I felt. The more I elevated my state of being the greater the experiences I witnessed became. During these new revelations I continued to discover the true meaning of love and was able to fully reconnect once again with the Beings of Light. Most of the questions I had through the course of my life had been answered, helping me to open the eyes of my heart even wider. With all these revelations, the intense push to show to others what we really are keeps growing in me.

Soon, people who were searching for a spiritual path started to appear in my life. I was grateful that I could share with them the universal messages of love, faith, trust, forgiveness, goodness, and Oneness. One person remarked, "God bless you because although you are a scientist, you can still see the light."

Today, grateful that I was able to see beyond surface reality and shift the way I perceived the world, all the resentment I had toward people such as my husband, family, coworkers, classmates, ex-lovers and myself has simply vanished and all that remains is love. Love has brought me to heal all my wounds and for the past seven years I have been free from depression and sickness. "With deep understanding comes Love and with True Love comes simultaneous forgiveness," the Beings of Light once told me. "There is no judgment in the eyes of the One who is True Love."

If you want to know the insights of all these profound revelations and learn more of the teachings of the Beings of Light, stay tuned, because I am here to share with you all these wonders in my upcoming writings.

Now, I know that I have always had the power to live a life filled with joy. By allowing ourselves to choose Joy and Love as the chief motivators in our lives, we are making the choice of being fully aligned with God and shining as Beings of Light. My life experience has revealed to me that there is not a need to die to go to Heaven, because Heaven is here and now. Stay connected to your truth, and give yourself the opportunity to rediscover and shine the Light that you already are.

"*In Lak'esh* (I am you)"

Acknowledgements

I deeply appreciate with all my heart each one of the incredible people that made this book shine like a polished jewel. Lana Cagle, Holly Garvin, Brandon Maeda, Lizzie Vance and D. Patrick Miller, I truly thank you for being part of this amazing journey, helping with your wisdom to shape every single page of this book. I am also grateful for the absolute support, patience and infinite love that I have received from my husband Mike and son David, whom I deeply adore. I profoundly appreciate as well, the unfailing love and care I have always received from my parents and sisters. Through the pages of this book, that I never thought I would ever write, I have tried to sketch the best I could how I have experienced and perceived life as part of this divine vehicle named Ingrid.

For me, this book represents a heavenly gift from God. Therefore, I am so honored and deeply grateful to serve as a vehicle for the Divine Universal Consciousness to manifest itself. However, I have not been the only one enjoying the writing of this book, for the Beings of Light have been with me shining every step of the way. I love to see how their light shines brightly every time I am typing the words that one day will bring light into the life of others.

Now, I actually sense that this book wanted to be written perhaps before I was even born. In the end everything is just a manifestation of a Universal Consciousness, leading us to awaken.

Made in the USA
Coppell, TX
21 August 2020

34169493R00144